WARFARE IN ANCIENT EGYPT

WARFARE IN ANCIENT EGYPT

BRIDGET MCDERMOTT

SUTTON PUBLISHING

First published in the United Kingdom in 2004 by
Sutton Publishing Limited · Phoenix Mill
Thrupp · Stroud · Gloucestershire · GL5 2BU

British Library Cataloguing in Publication Data
A catalogue record for this book is available from the British Library.

ISBN 0-7509-3291-0

Typeset in Garamond 11.5/15 pt.
Typesetting and origination by
Sutton Publishing Limited.
Printed and bound in England by
J.H. Haynes & Co. Ltd, Sparkford.

Contents

For Stephen and Delphi,
in memory of William M. Hicks

Acknowledgements

I would like to thank Abdullah Abdullah, Mohamed Hasan Ali and all the staff of the Antiquities Office, Luxor; Elham Aly of the Egyptian Museum, Cairo; Dr Sue D'Auria of the Museum of Fine Arts, Boston; Dr Catherine Bridonneau of the Musée du Louvre, Paris; Carolyn Graves-Brown of the University of Wales, Swansea; Professor Betsy Bryan and Vivian Davies of the British Museum, London; Dr Anna Maria Donadoni Roveri of the Museo Delle Antichita Egizie; Dr W.M. Haarlem of the Allard Pierson Museum, Amsterdam; Mrs Rosalind and Professor Jac Janssen; Dr Luc Limme and Donald Lowle of the University of Liverpool; Francesco Nicosia of the Musee Egizio di Firenze; Dr John Nunn; David Orman and the staff at John Rylands Library, Manchester; also the staff at both the Sydney Jones Library and the Archaeology Library at the University of Liverpool, and the British Library, London.

Further, I would like to express my gratitude to Dr William Peck, and Gabriele Pieke of the Pelizaeus-Museum, Hildesheim; to Dr J. Raven of the Rijksmuseum, and Dr Catherine Roehrig of the Metropolitan Museum of Fine Arts, New York; to Dr Bettina Schmitz, the Pelizaeus-Museum, Hildesheim; to Drs Ian Shaw, Christopher Eyre and Stephen Snape of Liverpool University. I am also indebted to John Taylor of the British Museum, John Waller of the Royal Armouries, Leeds, Claire Warrior of the Pitt-Rivers Museum, Oxford, and Pat Winker of the Department of Oriental Studies, the University of Liverpool.

For their assistance with travel scholarships, I would like to thank Richard S. Harwood and David Pepper and the Amarna Research Foundation, the Joan Allgrove McDowell Travelling Scholarship, and the University of Manchester Travel Scholarship Awards. I would especially like to thank Professor A.R. David for all her help and encouragement while I was researching material for this book.

On a personal level, many thanks to Nadine Balicki, David Beaumont, Jamie Bentham and Dr Stephen Buckley of Bristol University, Alison Chester, Paul, Poppy and Tom. Thanks, as always, to Dr Joann Fletcher of University College London, and the Fletcher family, Gary, Susan and Kate. Thank you to Joyce Filer of the British Museum and Sami Adib Gindi for his assistance in Khartoum. I would also like to express my gratitude to Professor Ken Kitchen of the University of

Liverpool and to the late Alan Schulman. Thanks to John Hill, Jonathan Hunt, W. Kendrick, Angie and Pat Mondino, Mo Plume, Michael Preston, Jason Semmens and Fiona Jane Wilson. For their contribution to the writing of this book I would like to express my gratitude to Stephen Jobling and Barbara McDermott.

Introduction

Modern records of ancient military history are largely dominated by the study of Greek warfare. Although much neglected, Egyptian military history too can provide scholars and the interested public with rich, unique and diverse information on ancient warfare. Three thousand years of continuous development of military arms and armour, beginning with the early predynastic culture (3200 BC) and culminating in the totalitarian supremacy of the New Kingdom (1552–1069 BC), can be systematically traced through military imagery. In addition, Egyptian weapons culture may itself be traced from the manufacture of flint hand-axes, wooden staves and stone bludgeons, to the introduction of the composite bow and the use of sophisticated and elegant weapons like the khepesh, long-sword and javelin. Aside from the purely military this book also provides a unique anthropological insight in that it uncovers the environmental and logistical factors that motivate groups of males to work or wage war in organised units and to act under elected command. It aims to show that several elements of military ritual and display have survived the early period and may be observed well into the New Kingdom phase – some of these themes can still be seen in modern Egypt in the form of stick-fighting and military ornamentation; some can be clearly identified among the aggressive displays of modern African tribesmen.

While the military achievements of the Greeks were recorded in epic poetry and literature, the Egyptians promoted their military achievements through art, myth and kingship. However, this did not mean that the Egyptians avoided literary reference; on the contrary, they celebrated their military strength through a prolific series of artistic and written records. While individual acts of valour were admired and rewarded, there is no evidence to suggest that the concept of honour was promoted through romantic literature or wisdom texts. The Egyptians achieved order (national security) through the prowess of the ruler, which meant that the state perpetuated grandiose images of war through royal iconography. The common soldier was depicted in order to display weapons and represent Egypt as a unified stronghold. In effect, individualism, or individual heroism, was considered an unproductive concept, and while the soldier was rewarded for bravery with land and material goods, his role was never overtly celebrated or distinguished through art. However, careful examination of the many different ways in which the soldier and his weapons are represented yields a rich store of information, predominantly, of course, about weapons in war.

Ancient Egyptian military technology has been subject to various methods of analysis that include the study of battlefield injuries. In the past, scholars sought to establish correlations between campaign accounts and the destruction of battle sites during the Late Bronze Age. Current studies, by contrast, tend to examine the political dimension of ancient warfare, and the results and rewards it brought the state and the economy. However, no major study has yet been undertaken on the individual experience of battle, and studies of the soldier, and his place within the social and religious structure of Egyptian society, are conspicuously absent. Our current knowledge of military technology in ancient Egypt is based on evidence derived from state representations, ancient technology, inscriptions and later records of military campaigns. Some scholars have attempted to analyse the role of weapons that belong to a single class, while others have established comparisons between weapons and tools excavated from Near Eastern sites. When weapons are addressed, they are often discussed only in terms of their function as possessions of the elite. In short, the connection between the soldier, his arms and armour and their representational significance is rarely made. Until now, for example, there has been no attempt to find out how the soldier handled and transported his weapons.

The ordinary soldier has often been ignored in studies of political history, military strategy, and the topography and ethnography of the ancient Near East. To make our task more difficult, evidence about the ancient Egyptian military is imbued with royal and religious propaganda, but with very little information on the common soldier. Although it is generally believed that a professional army did not exist until the New Kingdom phase (1552 BC), this book seeks to prove that the proficiency of the Egyptian military machine before this period has been seriously underestimated. Neglecting the role of the soldier ignores the basic component of that military system. Furthermore, in disregarding the role and the function of the weapon in combat, the historian fails to address the fundamental significance of arms. Warfare is intrinsic to human behaviour. It affects society as a whole and defines geographical, political and economic boundaries. Analysing the political structure of warfare while neglecting the individual roles of the men who fought only gives half the picture. With this book, I aim to not only redress the balance, but to present new material and so widen the perspectives of ancient Egyptian military studies.

This book offers, for what I believe is the first time, a complete record of pictorial representations of Egyptian soldiers and their weapons and so attempts both to challenge established academic works that have confined their exploration of the military to the ranks of the elite, and to place the common footsoldier and his arms within a chronological time-frame. It explores the depiction in art of the soldier and his arms and armour from the Predynastic Period until the 20th Dynasty, when numbers of known military reliefs decrease considerably. It also presents a detailed study of how weapons were manufactured and the response of the ancient Egyptians as they adapted to the technology of their enemies with brilliant precision. Here is a detailed examination of the arms of the footsoldier, and of how the state, or its officials, portrayed the lower ranks of the military. The ways in which the soldier used, marked and carried his weapons are described and, where possible, I have attempted to interpret the behaviour of the soldier on the battlefield and examine the aims of military representations.

The Egyptians did not portray definitive representations of the military. It is clear that where the depiction of the common soldier was concerned, the aim was to promote and display arms; for this reason, men are shown with fine equipment, and are often portrayed with an array of short and long-range weapons which would have been difficult to carry. Despite this, we can learn a great deal from examining the weapons carried by the soldier, for they tend to be executed with great attention to detail when compared with material remains. The military scenes examined below are classed in specific phases; with rare exception, the history of military records is contained within major phases of Egyptian history, leaving the so-called intermediate periods for the most part poorly documented. The Egyptians used the same images over long periods. Indeed, cultural images, or themes of national identity, especially those with military connotations or traditions, are adopted by many cultures both ancient and modern that share similar standards, symbols and motifs. Modern interpretations of these images highlight several questions. To this end, in many cases I have considered arms and military imagery within the context of the social and religious practices of comparative African societies who share a similar environment to that of the ancient Egyptians. Here, I refer especially to the Nuer, Dinka and Masai tribes; the latter, in particular, reveal striking similarities in dress, arms and military practices with ancient Egyptian warriors.

This book aims to present a definitive account of the Egyptian military to both the general reader and the military historian. It covers the political and cultural growth of the Egyptian state system and seeks to explain how a primitive society could evolve into a city state, maintain the security of its borders and acquire the wealth and technology that enabled it to resist foreign occupation over vast periods of time. Finally, the book investigates the imperial role of Egypt in the Near East and examines the policies of the New Kingdom warrior pharaohs who, by the year 1352 BC, had become the supreme rulers of the then known world.

ONE

Ancient Warfare

EGYPT IN PREHISTORY

As the northern ice cap began to melt, the grasslands of North Africa were inundated and reduced to isolated regions of pasturage and oases; water became scarce. Nomads who preyed on the game found in the forests and plains were forced to change their hunter-gatherer lifestyles. We can trace these nomadic peoples to 300,000 BC, during the Lower Paleolithic era, when there is clear evidence of a stone tool industry in Egypt. Paleolithic flints found there reveal that hand-axes were used as tools and weapons while prehistoric rock drawings show that antelope and elephant were hunted as game. As living creatures were drawn to the Nile Valley, people who had once hunted for their food now turned to the production of cereal crops. During this period the Nile Valley was a mass of swamp life; it was home to a variety of animals including fish, hippopotami, crocodiles, sheep and small desert game. All these creatures are depicted on objects of early Egyptian art.

The Nile Valley region was perfect for agriculture, and the land proved remarkably fertile. The Egyptians established an irrigation system which brought the rich alluvial mud of the Nile into the fields. Every year, in the middle of July, the river rose above its banks and flooded the land. Abundant harvests followed. The regularity of the Nile floods meant that large communities could be self-sufficient and people were no longer obliged to wander the plains in search of food. The annual cycle of crop sowings, flooding and harvest brought a rhythm to the lives of the people that also provided periods of leisure during which new cultural concepts were born. Animals were domesticated and a bartering system developed. The irrigation of the land was undertaken on a massive scale, and communities needed to cooperate. As the population began to increase, group leaders were appointed and the concept of hierarchy was established; settlements grew into large communities or districts, and worshipped local gods whose characteristics appeared on totems or banners. As the acquisition of land became more important and leaders began to vie for power, armed aggression came to be fuelled by politics rather than the accumulation of cattle.

EARLY WARFARE

The earliest known battle in the Near East occurred at Gebel Sahaba. The site, to the north of the Wadi Halfa in Egypt, was discovered in 1962. Here, a Stone Age massacre is known to have taken place in about 10000 BC. The excavated cemetery yielded the skeletons of fifty-two men, women and infants whose remains are carbon-dated to the Late Pleistocene Period. Qadan Period graves consisted of shallow oval pits, covered by rocks, and were decorated with the horns of cattle. Archaeologists discovered the remains of arrowheads in over 40 per cent of the graves (some flakes were found embedded in bone) and it seems likely that fatalities were the result of the multiple wounds inflicted on the victims. This event appears powerfully to contradict the widely held belief that hunter-gatherer groups were predominantly passive – and that violence occurred only at times of climatic instability and territorial expansion. It is also clear that early man used the bow and arrow as the world's first long-range weapon. Among nomadic tribes, or early settlements, men used arms to hunt game and kill other community members. As their communities developed, migrated and settled, organised bands of warriors waged war and attacked other small communities.

Primitive people living together in small or isolated groups did not compete for material goods, nor did their migrations over open territory inspire warriors to fight each other. Anthropological studies indicate that all males born to primitive communities were considered potential warriors. Tribal skirmishes had the purpose of acquiring women and cattle, and in return the warrior was expected to protect these commodities from alien tribesmen. There are already innumerable studies of warfare; this study will focus on the principle concepts of African warfare, namely that man was born a warrior, he fought for prestige, and acted as the guardian of his community.

In an attempt to analyse the early stages of Egyptian warfare, anthropological studies of tribal warfare have been examined and several parallels have been drawn with those that deal with the cattle cultures of Africa. Early representations from the Archaic Period – and, indeed, artistic representations of the later periods of ancient Egyptian history – illustrate themes that indicate a culture whose collective identity was heavily influenced by cattle rearing. However, as hunter-gatherer communities began to settle into agricultural lifestyles, permanent occupation gave rise to strong territorial bonds and, in addition to cattle, the tribe would seek to establish land-rights. Societies were drawn together into towns, and the process of urbanisation began. The tribe, no longer a predominantly warrior culture, appointed leaders and 'diplomats' who engaged in trade. New resources allowed the display of wealth and the construction of elaborate tombs that are common features of an emerging society. But their more violent past still manifested itself: during the formation of early states, blood sacrifice and cannibalism often became commonplace.

THE ARCHAIC PERIOD

The early populations of Egypt became farmers, artisans and officials. At an early date the calendar was developed, and the Egyptians created a tax system. Advances in writing meant that history was now being formed; during the Archaic Period writing was still in its infancy and it was to reach its classical stage during the Middle Kingdom. Manetho, an Egyptian priest who lived in the 3rd century BC, divided the history of Egypt into thirty-one dynasties, the earliest of which was marked by pharaonic rule. This system is still used by Egyptologists. The first two dynasties are classed as the Thinite Period, after This, a town in Upper Egypt. During the earliest phases of the Thinite Period the Egyptians were extending their borders and were already engaging in warfare with neighbouring peoples to the south and the west.

THE UNIFICATION OF EGYPT

A great change took place in Egypt around 3200 BC when the country was unified under one king. It was a time when great advances were made in cultural, political and military life. The Egyptians began to commission monumental architecture; their rulers were buried in elaborate tombs known as mastabas. These advances, made during a relatively short period, have led Egyptologists to speculate that the unification of Egypt, i.e. the amalgamation of the northern and southern regions, was the result of an invasion by as yet unidentified peoples.

Images carved on a predynastic object known as the Gebel el-Arak knife (Fig. 1) together with a wall painting from Tomb 100 (Fig. 2) at Hierakonpolis all have military themes, while their undoubted Mesopotamian influences once led

Fig. 2: A wall painting from Tomb 100 at Hierakonpolis. This archaic painting shows images that became iconographic during later periods of ancient Egyptian history, in particular the dueling figures of two males armed with shields and staves and a chieftain crushing the skulls of bound prisoners with a mace. *(Bridget McDermott/Glasgow City Museum and Art Gallery)*

scholars to believe that they depicted foreigners. (Egyptologists now disregard the idea that the master race, known as the 'followers of Hours', were non-Egyptian.) The warlike imagery carved on archaic objects, namely mace (Fig. 3), pottery and palettes was probably inspired by civil disturbances as the north and south struggled for dominance. The animals carved or painted on these objects, symbolise chaos; as in the natural world, the larger animals attack the weak. The animals are always quadrupeds placed in allegorical and turbulent scenes. Boats, too, often figure on ancient pottery; they represent the arrival of outsiders who bring disorder to an established nome or district. Several icons are included in these early military representations; a noted one shows an exotic beast tamed by a pair of human figures, an image complemented by that of a dominant chief who is shown in heroic pose, about to smash the skulls of shackled prisoners (Fig. 4).

Opposite: Fig. 1: The ivory handle of the Gebel el-Arak knife shows shaven-headed soldiers arriving by boat fighting with local tribesmen. They are armed with mace and staves. *(Joann Fletcher/ Louvre Collection, Paris)*

Fig. 3: The Scorpion Macehead from Hierakonpolis is a fine example of these large ceremonial objects that were often found in archaic deposits. It probably depicts King Narmer who unified Upper and Lower Egypt. The standards at the top of the mace represent the conquered enemies of the king. *(Bridget McDermott/Ashmolean Museum, Oxford)*

Detail from Tomb 100 at Hierakonpolis, showing the chieftan crushing the skulls of shackled prisoners, see Fig. 4, below left. (Bridget McDermott)

Fig. 4: This detail from Tomb 100 at Hierakonpolis shows the shackling and smiting of prisoners. The two warriors in the centre are armed with curved batons. *(Bridget McDermott)*

THE PYRAMID AGE

The Egyptian rulers adopted the epithet 'ruler of the two lands', a term that was retained throughout Egyptian history and which refers to the unification of the south and north under one Egyptian king. As Egypt became secure, land management flourished and the government implemented successful agricultural policies and irrigation techniques. The population of Egypt prospered and towns grew up creating permanent settlements along the Nile. Developments in calculus and writing meant that the Egyptians could erect monuments and organise armies.

Elaborate burials and funerary inscriptions are an important feature of Old Kingdom Egypt. The Old Kingdom begins with the 3rd Dynasty and is dominated by a series of kings who turned their attention to foreign expansion and the acquisition of wealth that would fund their elaborate tombs. Egypt was making scientific and technical advances, and by the time of the 4th Dynasty the king had established a trading system with neighbouring countries. The three great kings of that dynasty, Khufu, Khephren and Menkaure built pyramids on the site of the Giza plateau. At the beginning of the 5th Dynasty, Userkaf came to the throne. During this time, the sun god became pre-eminent in Egypt and thereafter kings took the title 'Son of Re'.

Gradually, power was passed to the noble families of Egypt. They built elaborate tombs in the vicinity of the pyramids which they had decorated to the highest standard. Inside, the walls were dominated by agricultural scenes and military reference was neglected. By the end of the 5th Dynasty central government was weakened by these nobles who established themselves in the role of nomarchs and were no longer accountable to the king.

Organised Warfare

During the ancient Egyptian Archaic Period (3300-3150 BC), a series of 'nomes' or towns began to grow up and trade along the Nile Valley; here, the divided cultures of the north and south have been identified through weapons and pottery found in their respective archaic graves. Conflicts that occur during the

Fig. 5: This magnificent spear, found in the tomb of Hemaka, is crafted from a single elephant tusk. *(Bridget McDermott/Egyptian Museum, Cairo)*

Archaic Period were initiated by urbanised communities who were familiar with writing. Military raids were recorded by the rulers of the 1st Dynasty (3150–2925 BC); these campaigns were commemorated in two rock cut inscriptions at Gebel Sheikh Suleiman in the south, while Egyptian rulers conducted Asiatic campaigns to secure their borders. Writings found on objects in ancient tombs dating from the 2nd Dynasty include the king's epithet 'conqueror of foreign lands', suggesting that military activity on Egypt's frontiers was probably a common occurrence. During this time, too, smiting scenes are regularly depicted on objects recovered from burial sites, while officials were buried in elaborate tombs; Hemaka, the chancellor of King Den, who conducted several Asiatic campaigns, was buried with a magnificent array of weapons, among them an ivory spear and hundreds of finely crafted arrows (Figs 5, 22 and 23).

Nor was the battlefield the only orbit for the soldier and his weapons. Throughout Egyptian history, mining expeditions were accompanied by the army, a practice evident from at least as far back as the 3rd Dynasty, when soldiers are known to have accompanied to southern Sinai parties sent to excavate copper and turquoise. By the 4th Dynasty there was even a permanent garrison at Buhen in the south of Egypt. Artistic representations of the period reveal strong military themes. Booty and captives listed on the Narmer Palette show the capture of 120,000 prisoners as well as large counts of cattle and livestock. Moreover, the kings of these early periods adopted names that reveal strong hunter-warrior themes – for example, the name of an early ruler, A-ha, means 'fighter' while the implication of the name Scorpion is obvious.

During the Old Kingdom (2700–2190 BC), the administrative system in Egypt had grown sophisticated enough to protect its borders, enabling trade and mining to flourish. Egypt had already established a time-honoured system of foreign relations that enabled it to trade and acquire goods. A standing army was never depicted within the canon of state iconography, and few military reliefs and inscriptions have survived from this period. While depictions from the great tombs of the Old Kingdom were dominated by domestic or agricultural themes, images of warfare were not commemorated through monumental art or architecture. Records of military events, however, have survived.

During the Old Kingdom Snoferu led military expeditions into Nubia where he crushed a revolt and captured prisoners and cattle – a recurrent feature of the hunter-warrior topos. The army of this period was composed of an organised body of men led by an appointed commander and was accompanied by large groups of non-military personnel, which probably included women. Minor campaigns were conducted by soldiers engaged on expeditions, and there are records of skirmishes with nomadic peoples. Commercial expeditions flourished from the 4th Dynasty when Egypt developed trading links with Lebanon and Syria. Also from the reign of Snoferu, the Egyptians established a sailing fleet; they made their first commercial contacts with the Aegean during the reign of Userkaf; expeditions to Byblos and Punt, and trade in the northern Mediterranean is thought to have occurred at least from the 5th Dynasty.

There are two important military texts dated to the Old Kingdom and revealed in the autobiographies of two soldiers, Harkuf and Weni. The soldier Weni, who served in the army of Pepy I, describes the precise and systematic actions of the army in the following way: 'When his majesty took action against the Asiatic sand-dwellers, he made an army of many tens of thousands from all of Upper Egypt'. Of the army he says: 'The army returned safe and sound, it had ravaged and flattened the land of the sand-dwellers, it had sacked their strongholds, it had cut down their figs and vines, it had burnt down their buildings, slain their troops by their tens of thousands, and carried off many of their soldiers as captives'.

At the end of the Old Kingdom power was gradually passed down through the central authorities to lesser officials in the form of tomb and land donations. The acquisition of power by landowners led to the development of a feudal system that would eventually result in civil war.

Warfare and Religion

In the Old Kingdom text known as Papyrus Westcar, the subjects of the king are described as the 'noble cattle' – a term that may have had its origins among cattle culture communities composed of warriors, women and holy men in which the functions of the priest and the warrior were totally integrated and symbiotic. Early initiation rites – still depicted in Old Kingdom funerary art – record a rite of passage in which young boys became tribesmen. This process could not be undertaken without an initiator, the holy man, without whose teaching boys could not become warriors. It is highly likely that the priest would direct the rite and through divination or prophecy he would act as intermediary between men and gods. Although the holy man had no role in skirmishing, he was responsible for any number of magical practices aimed at encouraging victory. In Egypt, as in other early cattle cultures, the priest or holy man would receive the prizes of war on behalf of the tribe or army, an act often accompanied by a ceremonial count of cattle and human prisoners, who were used respectively for meat and sacrifice.

As the apparatus of state developed and the gap between the tribe and the holy man widened, conflicts arose between officials of the administration and the priests who still acted as intermediaries between the ruler and his gods. Anthropological studies highlight the fact that early state formation is often characterised by rituals of blood sacrifice or cannibalism and point to the evidence of early Egyptian art, where men are shown bound and garrotted. Although we have little evidence of cannibalism in ancient Egypt, it is interesting to note that the practice is described in the Pyramid Texts, where violence and the consumption of human flesh are constant themes.

It is Khons who slew the lords, who strangles them for the king, and extracts that which is in their bodies. For he is the envoy who the king sends to bind. It is Shezmu who cuts them up for the king and who cooks for him a portion of them on his evening hearth-stones; it is the king who eats their magic and gulps down their spirits.

Depictions of early Egyptian settlers reveal typical themes that are still discernible among modern cattle cultures – where skirmishes that resulted from cattle raids were more common than territorial disputes. Indeed, animal motifs played a significant role during all periods of Egyptian military history, and so far it has not been possible to distinguish between the image of the hunter and that of the warrior. Cattle had enormous economic importance for early settlers, and form the basis for exchange and inter-community relations; they were the major food source, with meat and milk products also constituting important offerings during religious rituals. Leather was used for clothing, blankets and protective covers, tools were manufactured from bone, and dung was used as fuel. It is not surprising that a community came to look upon its cattle as its primary resource. Indeed, cattle, and the sacrifice of animals formed the very basis of Egypt's early religious system. Of these early cultures, the anthropologist Evans-Pritchard observed, 'their social idiom is a bovine idiom'.

The significance of cattle and their incorporation into warrior symbolism is evident, too, from creative remains. It is probable that early images of the Egyptian warrior appear in the form of dancers painted on predynastic pottery (Fig. 6). Here, the dancers are shown with their arms raised to imitate horns. Interestingly, this type of dance is still performed in Africa, and the image of the dancing warrior, his arms raised, is found on the shields of modern tribesmen. Often the dancer is being chased by men carrying nets, or is accompanied by a hunter-warrior who is armed with either a short or a long

Fig. 6: In this scene tribesmen are shown wearing elaborate headdresses, with their arms raised to imitate cattle horns. The object hanging above them is a typical pre-dynastic shield decorated with animal tails. The shield was made of leather, which was attached to a wooden frame. *(Bridget McDermott)*

stick. The figures often have male genitalia. The modern-day funeral practices of the Luo tribe of the Mara district of northern Tanzania may shed some light on these scenes. Here, armed warriors wearing tall headdresses play a major role in the funeral of a tribesman. During the funeral, the spirit of the deceased is symbolically transferred into the body of a living cow, and the warriors dance to drive the spirit back into the bush, where it is released. As these modern warriors don their headdresses, early Egyptian hunter-warriors did likewise, and were often depicted with masks. During acts of warfare covering the face is thought to intimidate the enemy, or allow a man to identify himself with a totem image. While it is clear that the early hunters hoped to imbue themselves with the spirit of their prey by wearing masks, these also functioned as early symbols of Egyptian domination or, in a religious context, were worn to induce a spiritual communion between the wearer and the gods.

The initiation rites of tribal man served to distinguish the role of the male from that of the women of the tribe. While women were seen as figures of fecundity, the warrior was often associated with death. All tribal cultures

Fig. 7: This scene was carved on the walls of a tomb of an unknown Old Kingdom occupant. It is probably a ritual of transition or an initiation ceremony into warriorhood. While the leading figure wears a mask and headdress, others carry batons, one in the shape of a human hand. This type of baton was adopted by both the army and the police. (Bridget McDermott/British Museum Collection)

employ rituals that celebrate the transitions that boys make to manhood and there are several themes that link these ceremonies. Often the boy's head is partially shaved in order to re-create the prenatal state that indicates rebirth. During the rite the boys are naked, and are reclothed after the ceremony. Ritual beatings and taunts are common, usually taking place within an initiation hut where the boys are secluded prior to the event. At the culmination of the initiation, established members of the tribe drag the boys from the hut as a symbol of their rebirth. These events find their historical precursor in representations on several early Old Kingdom tomb walls (Fig. 7).

MILITARY IMAGES OF THE EARLY PERIOD AND THE OLD KINGDOM

It is thought that primarily nomadic primitive people existed for centuries without the pressure to compete, and that the desire to do so is inherent in the nature of settled groups that depend on land for their survival. Long-term occupation has a strong effect on the human psyche producing a strong sense of ownership and permanence, which stimulates the development of religious centres, the need to establish ancestral lines and to record events. Armed aggression, already highly developed during the 1st Dynasty, originated among small communities slowly developing into statehood. These communities competed and exchanged goods. In Egypt these concepts are relevant to wealthy communities who produced fine tombs for their leaders. These burial places were decorated with emblems of victory and equipped with luxury goods.

The pottery and grave goods of the ancient Egyptians were decorated with emblems that were often associated with warfare or religion. During the establishment of the state economy, the Egyptians displayed elaborate goods as icons of wealth. In Egypt this meant that tombs were equipped with decorated objects that reflected state ideology – subsequently, representations show the emergence of the 'heroic attitude' in art, namely, the image of a commander smiting his enemies. Here the Egyptians often depicted the ruler grasping a group of males by the hair with one hand, while in the other he grips a mace that is raised above their skulls. The theme of triumph over one's enemies is powerfully presented, too, at the tomb of an archaic chieftain, Tomb 100 at Hierakonpolis (Fig. 4). This is decorated with a remarkable wall painting that shows a row of fettered prisoners accompanied by a man dressed in animal skins. The man, who is shown smiting his prisoners with a mace, is depicted in priestly attire. Although the painting contains vestigial images of a tribal system, it also shows the basic principles of an evolving economic culture.

Palettes

Military themes were also carved on to large ceremonial palettes and mace-heads (Fig. 3). Cosmetic palettes, originally used for mixing eye paint, were exaggerated in size and decorated with scenes of hunting and warfare. The imagery carved on these palettes is frequently gruesome, highlighting acts of mutilation, decapitation or the loss of eyes. In several scenes the eyes are emphasised, as is the way the enemy is often shown looking over his shoulder towards the victorious ruler. The Egyptians placed these palettes in early burials as symbols of regeneration – the state in which the eyes are opened. Zoomorphic or oval in shape, Egyptian palettes were most probably designed to commemorate or record historical events and were often found in predynastic burials along with large inscribed mace. An important object of this type, the Narmer Palette, is our earliest example yet of the way the Egyptians placed their art images into multiple configurations or registers, a technique which may emphasise the new sense of organisation that was required by an emergent society united under one king. Various animal and human motifs are used on the Narmer Palette. The traditional image of the king holding a mace above the head of his northern enemy dominates one side, while the other reveals the king in the form of a bull about to destroy the walls of an enemy city with his horns. Here, the king is proceeded by standard bearers of various provinces. A series of decapitated prisoners is shown, their heads placed between their legs. On the lower fragment of the palette a fortress, complete with bastions, is depicted. The Narmer Palette shows, too, a group of warriors carrying emblems used to distinguish a unit by its affiliation with a town or village. The role of the standard-bearer alone may indicate complex developments in military organisation.

Fig. 8: The Hunter's Palette reveals strong military themes, although here the hunting scene acts as an allegory. The soldiers shown on the palette carry throwsticks, bows, a pair of spears and a double macehead. *(Bridget McDermott/British Museum Collection)*

Fig. 9: Detail from the Hunter's Palette showing soldiers stalking lions. *(Bridget McDermott)*

Left and opposite: Fig. 10: This New Kingdom scene from Medinet Habu may be compared with that on the Hunter's Palette, although they are almost 2,000 years apart. Both scenes show warriors brandishing similar weapons and tethering ropes. Traditionally the king and his soldiers were shown hunting lions and bulls after a victorious campaign. *(Bridget McDermott/ Louvre, Paris and British Museum Collection)*

The Hunter's Palette (Figs 8–9) is generally considered to be a commemorative object that may depict the victory of the south over the north of Egypt. On it young males carry long-range weapons; used in military manoeuvres, these weapons were clearly more complex than those used during hand to hand skirmishes. The palette is decorated with animals and bovine deities. The lion drawing her cub take a central role in the narrative. The lion, the metaphorical image of the enemy chief, is pierced by arrows; he is pursued by phyles of soldiers armed with bows, spears, axes, throwsticks and pear-shaped mace. The men are divided into two sections, each division having a separate role in the 'hunt'. As on the Narmer Palette, the men carry standards that affiliate the group with a district or corps. The symbiotic relationship between hunting and military images on Egyptian palettes is clear. Ironically, this early example of military imagery dated to 3100 BC, acts as a facsimile for the last grandiose depiction of the New Kingdom army in 1186 BC. The scenes on the Hunter's Palette and the victory scenes from the 19th Dynasty Temple of Medinet Habu reveal a striking similarity – both depict soldiers stalking game (Fig. 9). The congruence between the two pieces highlights the enduring connection between Egyptian military art and the hunter-warrior theme.

The Battlefield Palette (Fig. 10) shows men with Libyan features being attacked by both lions and vultures. The slain soldiers are depicted on the

battlefield, their twisted bodies carved into impossible contortions. The scene is rendered in the past tense, the field abandoned by the army – our earliest example of the carnage of war being illustrated by carrion birds plucking out the eyes of the executed prisoners. Significance is placed on the mutilation of the body, an abomination to the Egyptians who placed great emphasis on the preservation of the flesh.

Pottery

A large number of Egyptian pots were painted with a series of predynastic emblems (Fig. 11). They are often decorated with the images of dancing figures. Some representations reveal a bovine deity – perhaps an early form of the goddess Hathor. Similar figures are executed with male genitalia, and wear feathers in their hair. These dancing figures, who frequently occur among military images of the Middle and New Kingdoms, are accompanied by musicians who provide a marching rhythm by beating clappers (Figs 11 and 12). Clappers – an instrument still used in modern Africa – are always connected to cattle cultures; they appear at funerals and during rites of manhood when they are played before a group of warriors engaged in a cattle dance. The dance is

Fig. 10: Scenes from the Battlefield Palette highlight the deep horror the Egyptians felt regarding the physical desecration of the body. The lion represents the victorious king mauling the enemy. The vultures tear at the flesh of the enemy soldiers as they lie dying on the battlefield. *(Bridget McDermott/Ashmolean Museum, Oxford and British Museum Collection)*

reminiscent of those shown on archaic pottery, where men rotate their bodies, with their arms held above their heads in the shape of cattle horns. In another scene with a hunter-warrior theme, a male, shown in the cattle pose with his hands raised above his head, is being speared by a second male who carries a large body shield (Fig. 13). In addition, fragmentary images are often found on broken shards dated to the Predynastic Period. A fragment from Hierakonpolis shows a warrior with a mace and stave while other examples reveal early images of bowmen or marching soldiers who wear quivers on their backs.

Models and Masks

The oldest extant military model in the world, found at Diospolis Pava in Egypt, reveals two warriors placed behind an enclosure wall (Fig. 14). In this predynastic model, the soldiers appear to be naked. Their faces, shown peering from the wall, seem flat and could almost be described as mask-like, and masks

Figs 11 and 12: Both male and female figures are shown engaged in a cattle dance on ancient pottery. The male figures are accompanied by comrades who beat clappers. (See New Kingdom fragment Fig. 119.) *(Bridget McDermott/British Museum Collection)*

Fig. 13: In this early representation on a predynastic vase, a dancing male is shown being speared by a warrior. *(Bridget McDermott/Ashmolean Museum, Oxford)*

are, in fact, known from this period. A mask is worn by a hunter-warrior figure on the Ostrich Palette, while a lion-headed mask is also worn by an individual who appears in an initiation scene from an Old Kingdom mastaba tomb (Fig. 7). The skulls of the soldiers on the Diospolis Pava model bear indentations, and it is highly likely that they once wore a headdress or wig – emblems designed to create a striking or threatening effect when their faces peered above the wall of an early enclosure (Fig. 14).

Tomb Decoration

Several tombs of the Old Kingdom reveal images of what was once thought to be a children's game known as 'bringing in the prisoner'. Here, a group of males is shown armed with staves; they lead a bound man in a traditional processional fashion. The Old Kingdom mastaba tombs often depict initiation scenes that highlight a boy's transition to manhood. The illustrations reveal a group of human figures armed with staves. In one scene three individuals are shown inside a hut; while one individual lies prostrate on the floor, the men behind him are shown standing. A person, placed at the door of the hut, encourages the fallen boy to raise himself and emerge (Fig. 7). Such scenes are always accompanied by images of wrestling and stick-fighting. In fragments from the British Museum (Fig. 7), the boys are armed with staves shaped in the form of the human hand – these batons were used by both the military and the police during all periods of Egyptian history.

Wall paintings in Old Kingdom tombs sometimes provide Egyptologists with information about military technology. The tomb of Inta contains an early siege scene that is dated to the Old Kingdom period and is a complex depiction of a fortified city protected by bastions (Fig. 15). In this scene Egyptian soldiers are shown climbing a siege ladder which they had placed against a city wall. The narrative has no sequential place in time and all images occur within one spatial fragment. However, the Egyptian artist has managed to express a past tense, for although archers are absent from the painting, the bodies of soldiers, probably Asiatic, are shown pierced with arrows. These wounded soldiers are depicted being executed by soldiers armed with axes. Within the city walls, the population

Fig. 14: The Diospolis Pava fragment is the world's oldest military model. It shows a fortified structure. Here two soldiers, in their role as guards, are seen peering over a wall. (*Bridget McDermott/ Ashmolean Museum, Oxford*)

is shown under siege, people are being attacked by soldiers while others are beaten to the floor – the prostrate bodies bearing a striking resemblance to those twisted figures shown on the base of the Narmer Palette. In the lower register of the scene the prisoner procession shows warriors being herded away like cattle.

In another Old Kingdom siege scene, this time from the tomb of Khamehesit (Fig. 16), a siege ladder that was rolled on wheels is positioned against the wall of a fort. Egyptian soldiers, who usually carry weapons in the bands of their kilts, are shown hacking at the walls of the city with their axes. In this way, the image of the hoe, which often appears on predynastic palettes, was placed above the enclosure scene as a symbol of forced entry; the hoe was often used in this way, to indicate the hacking down of mud brick walls (Fig. 31).

Other Old Kingdom tombs, such as that of Ptah-Hotep at Saqqara, contain a series of representations that include wrestling, stick-fighting and rope climbing – all of which may have a military subtext. Two fragments recovered from separate Old Kingdom tombs are carved with a group of soldiers who carry cylindrical stave cases. While one remains fragmentary, the second shows a troupe of soldiers accompanied by scribes, a detail of organisation that is not generally associated with the Old Kingdom army (Fig. 17).

Fig. 15: This scene from the tomb of Inta at Deshashe shows the enemy wounded by bowmen. The soldiers wield hatchets as they lay siege to an enemy city. *(Bridget McDermott)*

Fig. 16: This detail from the tomb of Khamehesit shows the Egyptians using a siege ladder to gain access to a fortified town and their Asiatic enemies. The soldiers are shown with their axes tucked into their kilts. Later the Egyptians would design their axes with straps so that they could be worn around the body. *(Bridget McDermott)*

SOLDIERS AND ARCHERY

Bows

The bow is the most ancient weapon known to man; although developed in pre-history, its use can be positively identified around 10,000 BC, when its capacity to inflict injury on man is attested. Egyptian bows were plied during the earliest recorded periods using materials such as sycamore and lemonwood, sinew and horn. Predynastic bows were designed in both simple and composite forms. The design of the simple bow, which is still used in modern Africa, shares with its ancient Egyptian counterpart a peculiar type of limb arch. It retains a rounded form, while the extremities are joined, producing a circumflex wooden limb. Another type of bow was constructed with antelope horn which acted as a con-nective fragment. A number of small horn bows have been found in Egypt, but Egyptologists generally class these examples as votive models, and while remains of predynastic bows have been excavated, they are rare. Examples, which include broken wooden bow-tips from predynastic sites prove that bows, whether for ordinary use or as amulets, were painted and decorated in totem colours or insignia.

Ancient bowstrings exhibit the self-same features of modern gut lines. The earliest example of a gut bowstring is dated to the Badarian Period, where the bowstring was described as a 'thong of animal tissue'. There is no pictorial evidence to suggest that the bow was crafted with string notches.

Only a small number of artistic representations of the predynastic warrior and his bow are known. However, archers are portrayed as hunter-warriors in scenes of the Archaic Period with a total of seven archers appearing on the Hunter's Palette (Fig. 8–9). In this piece the archer plays the most significant role within the narrative. Featured at the vanguard of the action, he is the first man to approach the enemy-prey in an attempt to bring him down. All the archers are armed with maces, weapons which were traditionally used to dispatch or finish off wounded enemy soldiers.

The practice of placing archery equipment among ancient Egyptian funerary goods was established and cultivated during the Old Kingdom. Excavated examples of Old Kingdom bow fragments are rare. However, some examples have survived from Asyut, together with their bowstrings (Fig. 18). Two long bows from Asyut, which are dated to the 6th Dynasty, are housed in the British Museum collection, while remnants housed in the Pitt-Rivers Museum, Oxford, probably belonged to the oldest recovered horn-bow in the world.

During the Old Kingdom the long bow (Fig. 19) was used for both hunting and military purposes. Old Kingdom bows were slightly curved and crafted without string nodules. During the 6th Dynasty the bow is figured with re-curved ends and rare examples of string attachments are known. Strings continued to be fashioned from twisted gut, a type which is clearly emphasised on the bows of Old Kingdom archers where the soldiers of Cheops, the builder of the Great Pyramid at Giza, are shown firing their bows (Fig. 20). The depiction of Cheops' archers illustrates a faction of men undertaking formal and well-drilled action. The piece was originally designed to portray a unit of archers, all of whom were uniform in movement, suggesting that the archer corps acted as a well-organised division. Literary attestations that date to this period deal with the slaughter of soldiers: 'the [hostile] hearts are held off [?], the bow-men who are in the (field) are slaughtered'. The god Horus is often associated with acts of military precision and was identified as an elite archer, being addressed as 'Horus the Shooter'. One inscription states: 'Bring the two Eyes of Horus – a "iwnt" bow. I am he who draws the bowstring as Horus and who pulls the cord as

Fig. 18: The string of this 6th Dynasty bow remains in its original state, looped and then pulled taut around the bow limb. *(Bridget McDermott/ British Museum Collection)*

Osiris'. It is often the case that bowmen can be identified amid commemorative scenes wearing a single or double feather upon the head. Soldiers from all periods of Egyptian history wear head adornments, but feathers have a special significance to bowmen whose representations adopt the double feathers from the Predynastic Period onwards.

Although there are few representations of archers being deployed in scenes of offensive action dating from the Old Kingdom, the presence of bowmen is clearly emphasised in a siege scene from Deshashe (Fig. 15). While archers are not shown at the locale, it is evident that these units had been used to bring down enemy soldiers, creating a rare tension in the narrative. The image of the archer is included, too, among hieroglyphic signs; here, held upright in the hands of kneeling archers, both strung and unstrung bows are depicted.

Fig. 19: This previously unpublished fragment is undated but is likely to have been crafted during the 5th or 6th Dynasty. It shows a row of archers marching with long bows and carrying arrows in their hands. *(Bridget McDermott/Egyptian Museum, Cairo)*

Fig. 20: The bowmen of Cheops, the builder of the Great Pyramid, are shown in this beautifully preserved and unique Old Kingdom fragment. Here, the twisted gut of the bowstrings can still be seen. (Bridget McDermott/ Egyptian Museum, Cairo)

Arrows

The earliest evidence for the use of arrows during acts of war or conflict originates from the Qadan area. Examinations conducted on the skeletal remains recovered from this site indicate fatal arrow wounds. The military role of the bow and arrow has no tangible origin in prehistory; however, it is without doubt the earliest projectile weapon known to man. As small communities developed around the Nile Valley during this period there was a need for both hunting and military weapons. With the exception of advances in metallurgy during ancient Egyptian military history the manufacture of arrows fails to incorporate any radical changes in design. Indeed, from the New Kingdom Period we find examples of predynastic arrows being reused in conjunction with 18th Dynasty bows.

Although arrow shafts were hafted in wood, reed remained the most accessible material to the ancient Egyptian arrow maker. Arrow shafts crafted from pine and acacia have been examined; they are bound by thread, and often show evidence of secured barbs. The arrowhead was secured to the shaft by binding or tang, the reed head was often secured with thread to prevent the arrow shaft from splitting. The tang had to be very long in proportion to the head, so that side pressure did not exert too much leverage and split the reed. Where socket heads were required for arrow tips, wood was occasionally used.

Flint was the most common commodity used in the manufacturing of arrowheads (Fig. 21). Flint arrowheads dated to the Badarian Period were often tanged. The fine craftsmanship of flint-heads may be examined among existing remains. A wide range of styles and designs is evident, particularly among large groups of arrowheads. Examples of bone, wood and copper arrowheads have all been recovered; while crystal arrowheads are rare, remains of these have been recovered from the royal tombs of the 1st Dynasty.

The remains of archery equipment found in the tomb of Hemaka provide examples of variegated arrow types discovered within a single group. These include large groups of arrows that were tipped with bone (Fig. 22); others were, decorated with blue and red bands, were barbed and fletched with gum and thread. An arrow found in this tomb is tipped with the jaw of a tiny fish (Fig. 23). They almost always show evidence of nock incisions. The arrows varied in length from 480 to 550mm; they were gathered in differently sized bundles ranging from collections of 78 to 122 staves. Another group, composed of an assortment of different arrow types, was found in a leather quiver. The cache consisted of groups of 42, 79 and 8 arrows, each group bound with strips of linen. Among Middle Kingdom tomb scenes, arrows were frequently shown baled in this manner.

There are plenty of remains which provide evidence of the materials and manufacture of predynastic arrowheads and arrow-shafts. Petrie, in his detailed examination of predynastic arrowheads included more than eleven variants.

Fig: 21: This flint arrowhead is a fine example of the delicate craftsmanship employed by the Old Kingdom Egyptians when manufacturing arrowheads. Stone, wood, ebony and even crystal arrowheads have been dated to this period. *(Bridget McDermott/Manchester Museum Collection)*

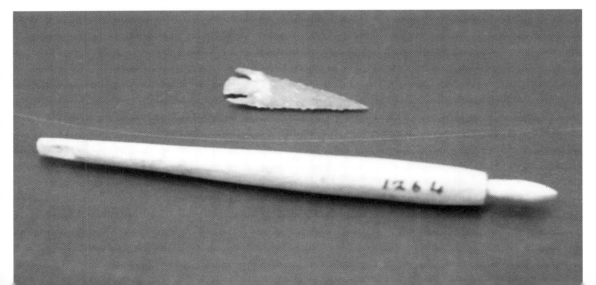

Fig. 22: These long elegant ivory arrowheads were found in the tomb of Hemaka. The arrowheads are fixed into reed shafts and cemented with resin. *(Bridget McDermott /Egyptian Museum, Cairo)*

Egyptologists have suggested that the design of the arrowhead was adapted for a specific purpose, that blades, crafted with barbs, were designed for piercing hide, while forked tips were used for hunting birds; it is quite clear that forked arrows were also used in battle (Fig. 24). Arrows were also often designed with long wooden points, which were painted with various identification marks using black pigmentation scarred with gypsum.

Academics have proposed explanations to account for the pigmentation commonly found on arrow tips of this period. For instance, these markings may have served to identify arrows coated with poison. Groups of ivory arrowheads, found among the remains of the 1st Dynasty tomb of Djer, are stained with red ochre, which some scholars have suggested might have been an attempt to work sympathetic magic. However, poisoned arrow tips are commonly used in modern Africa. It is quite possible that the Egyptians, who worked with vegetable alkaloids, snake and scorpion venoms, used poisons whose properties have yet eluded modern analysis.

The earliest representations of archers armed with arrows include an engraving from the Wadi Hammamat which reveals the image of a warrior

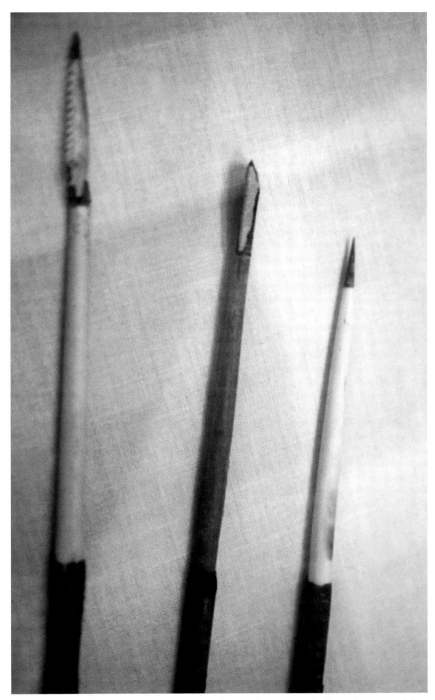

Fig. 23: These three arrows from the tomb of Hemaka are made from bone, and from the jaw of a tiny fish. A dark pigment can still be seen on the tip, which may indicate the use of poisoned arrowheads. *(Bridget McDermott/Egyptian Museum, Cairo)*

armed with a short curved bow, while a stele from the Archaic Period shows the figure of a male armed with both bow and mace. Among remains from the 1st Dynasty site at Abydos a hunter is depicted accompanied by hounds. On the Hunter's Palette described earlier, the archer is depicted preparing to shoot transverse arrowheads (Fig. 9), and he is armed with three arrows. In scenes from this palette the attacking warriors have established their position and are depicted with arrows already poised in their bows. The wounding of a Semite soldier pierced by this type of arrow is depicted on a palette fragment housed in the Metropolitan Museum of Art (Fig. 24).

During the Old Kingdom, there are no variations in the style and materials that were used during predynastic fletching. Soldiers and royal persons in hunting and military scenes are often depicted engaged in the process. Arrows are included in the military scenes from the tomb of Inta at Deshashe (Fig. 15), where they are shown as inanimate objects, having already pierced the upper and lower limbs of enemy soldiers. To date, there are few examples of artists illustrating the velocity of arrows in flight.

Before the development of gunpowder, the archer was often placed in the ranks of the elite, a practice clearly adopted by the ancient Egyptian military. During later periods, archers were often shown taking part in ceremonial processions, but during the Old Kingdom, military role and rank are seldom portrayed. Archers were included in royal ceremonies, where they were employed to ward off the enemies of Egypt in a ritual that included the shooting of an arrow at each cardinal point.

Fig. 24: A Semite soldier is pierced with a transverse arrowhead. *(Bridget McDermott/Metropolitan Museum of Art)*

Fig. 25: On this archaic fragment three warriors perform a typical military salute with the hand pressed to the breast. They carry long cylindrical quivers on their backs. *(Bridget McDermott/ Egyptian Museum, Cairo)*

Quivers

The remains of quivers have been excavated from archaic tombs. Crafted from panels of stitched leather, these quivers contained varying quantities of arrows, ranging from five to seventy-nine. The quivers were also designed to contain wooden staves. Artistic interpretations of the quiver are rare from the Archaic Period; however, the hunter-warrior figures on the Hunter's Palette carry quivers on their backs (Figs 8 and 9). Quivers are clearly illustrated, too, on the backs of early warriors on a small predynastic fragment now housed in Cairo Museum (Fig. 25).

Although it is possible to date the use of the quiver from the Predynastic Period, there are few material remains or artistic representations of these objects dated to the Old Kingdom. A possible exception is a dyed leather quiver discovered in Egypt. Knotted cords, which are still attached to the opening of the case, drew the leather opening together (Fig. 26). This quiver is similar in appearance to the remains found in the tomb of Hemaka and also to the cylindrical cases carried by the soldiers depicted on an Old Kingdom fragment which reveals unparalleled representations of a quiver designed to carry staves (Fig. 17).

Quivers were also crafted from plant fibre. They were designed with a belt that was worn over the shoulder and across the breast. The strap crossed to the

Above and below: Fig. 26: This leather quiver was dyed and then stitched into a cylindrical form. It was crafted with a drawstring top that is knotted several times around the opening. *(Bridget McDermott/British Museum Collection)*

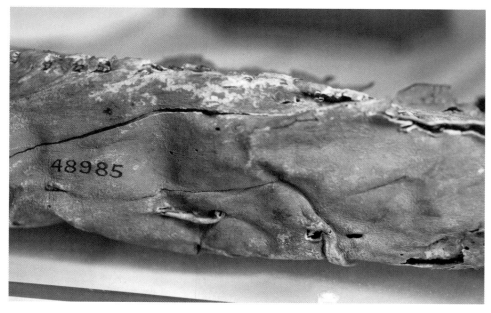

Fig. 17: The Lisht Marine Fragment reveals a well-drilled and organised unit on the march. The soldiers are accompanied by a military scribe and are equipped with staves which were carried in long cylindrical quivers. *(Bridget McDermott/Metropolitan Museum of Art)*

opposite side of the body so that the arrow or stave could be drawn from beneath the arm. Strings, or a hood cover, which remained attached by means of a tag or thong, were used to close the case.

SOLDIERS AND HATCHETS

The earliest tools and weapons of the Paleolithic Period were manufactured in the form of bifacial fragments or hand axes. These objects were first mounted on sticks and used in the familiar hatchet form around 45000 BC.

Axes were used throughout Egyptian history in both functional and ceremonial contexts and model and amuletic axes have been recovered from predynastic sites. The role of the axe in iconography remains complex. In African mythology the axe is often associated with the mattock, and was frequently adopted as a symbol of leadership and authoritative speech. During both the Archaic and Old Kingdom Periods the mattock continued to be represented in scenes illustrating the destruction of city walls. During the New Kingdom, hatchets were depicted in identical contexts when they were used for hacking down fort entrances (Fig. 89).

Although there are no early representations of males armed with hatchets, they can be seen among hieroglyphs dated to this period. A comprehensive typology of Old Kingdom axes has been established with regard to material remains. However, it is often difficult to distinguish battle axes among the common tools of this period. During the Old Kingdom, axes were represented in battle scenes from the tomb of Khamehesit at Saqqara where axes with crescent blades and curved hafts are shown tucked into the kilts of soldiers depicted on siege ladders (Fig. 16). Socket axes were also manufactured during this period, but no remains of these weapons have been found. The hatchet also appears in scenes from the tomb of Inta at Deshashe (Fig. 15). Here, they are shown being operated with single and double handed propulsion.

SOLDIERS AND SPEARS

The spear was a principal weapon of ancient man and its use can be dated to 70000 BC. As an offensive weapon its longevity is unparalleled in the field of both hunting and warfare. Subsequently, the spear has been retained throughout centuries of military cross-cultural evolution until the twentieth century when it was used in the form of a bayonet.

Included among the arms of the early warriors of Egypt, the spear was used as a short and mid-range weapon. The spear shaft was made of reed or wood and tipped with a flint blade. The Egyptians also manufactured a blade now known as the fish-tail lance head (Fig. 27). Although its purpose remains unclear, the blade may have had ceremonial functions – despite their use as objects of violation, various weapons came to be revered as mythological icons. The blades were multi-functional. An example of a fish-tail lance head, discovered with a cord wound around the blade, was obviously projectile in nature and may originally have been secured to a lance-shaft. Although this type of blade may have been employed as a spearhead, it was also used in the form of a short sword or dagger.

From the beginning of the Dynastic Period, around 3050 BC, metal processing techniques were being continuously developed and refined. Copper spearheads were crafted, perforated and bound to the spear shaft, albeit with materials we cannot identify.

Fig. 27: Many fish-tail lance heads have survived from the early period. Although they may have been multi-functional, only one clear indication of their use has been found in the form of a knife or dagger. However, this example was found with a cord and may have been a projectile weapon. *(Bridget McDermott/Ashmolean Museum, Oxford)*

The only known surviving predynastic spear was discovered among the contents of the tomb of Hemaka and it was probably ceremonial in nature. The spear is constructed from a wooden shaft, its blade crafted from an elephant tusk. The tusk was inserted into the shaft and secured by two copper nails which pass through each side of the base.

Early warriors relied on simple spears crafted from reed or wood which were tipped with flint. It is probable that a variation of the spear, the sharpened stave, was used for both hunting and warfare. Early representations in the Nile Valley include the figure of a male piercing the body of his enemy with a spear (Fig. 13). The traditional role of the spear in military conceptualisation is identified for the first time on the Hunter's Palette, where warriors are shown armed with pairs of spears (Figs 8 and 9). This scene reveals the rudimentary prototypical image of the Egyptian infantryman in phyle, a representation that would become one of the most commonly recurring features of military iconography during subsequent periods of ancient Egyptian history. There are four clear depictions of the spear. In each case the owner carries a throwstick as an auxiliary weapon.

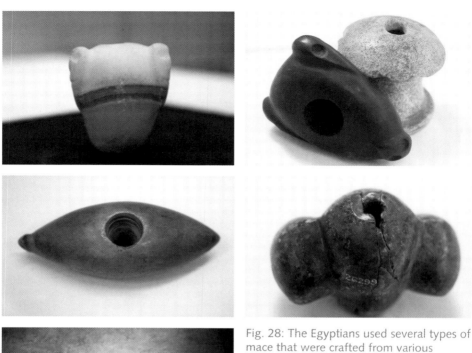

Fig. 28: The Egyptians used several types of mace that were crafted from various materials such as wood, stone and clay. Here, examples of notched, oval and spool shaped mace can be seen. The pear-shaped macehead (left) is a rare example of a weapon still mounted on its original stave. The Egyptians often decorated the macehead, and the cross, painted on the top of the mace, is a typical feature. *(Bridget McDermott/Liverpool University Museum)*

SOLDIERS AND MACE

There is a prolific variation in macehead design throughout all periods of Egyptian history (Fig. 28). The maceheads were crafted from various materials such as stone and clay; the head is sometimes designed with notches or protrusions, and is often carved with animal or human motifs. Predynastic mace may be described as discoid, pear shaped, diamond headed, spool shaped, oval or round. They are often decorated with motifs, the most common being a cross that is added to the apex.

During the later periods, the mace was associated with celestial fortifications and appears in texts from the Temple of Edfu as the deity, 'The Great White'. The mace was included in early religious iconography; it was often displayed in the talons of a falcon among scenes of siege warfare, where they were used to portray the crushing of walled towns or fortifications. Considering that it has been described as *the* characteristic weapon of the Predynastic Period, the mace plays a surprisingly minor role within the context of military art. It has never been found depicted during hand-to-hand combat. The military significance of the mace is impossible to define. Their martial context aside, the quantity and variation of design among these objects suggest the establishment of a coherent trading system. However, the mace was a clumsy object, and the disproportion of its weight against the shaft made it liable to fracture. The stave, evenly distributed and equally as brutal, was certainly the stronger weapon.

On the Hunter's Palette, six hunter-warrior figures are shown armed with mace, each carrying the mace in conjunction with the bow or the spear (Fig. 8). The weapon is always raised above the warrior's shoulder in the traditional smiting pose. The renditions on the Hunter's Palette also indicate the use of the double mace. Employed as a subsidiary weapon, the mace served to finish off wounded animals or enemy soldiers. In its role as a crushing weapon, it became a symbol of absolute dominance.

While the mace is apparently omitted from duelling scenes in paintings discovered at Tomb 100 at Hierakonpolis, it does, however, appear in a prototypical scene, where it is wielded by a warrior who is shown smiting prisoners, albeit this scene is clearly removed from the realm of actual combat (Fig. 4 drawn detail). In view of the importance of this tomb, one would expect the mace, if it were valued as a weapon of war, to be included among combat scenes. During this early phase, the mace may have been assimilated with heraldic images of royal domination and rightful rule — it is used in modern times in an identical fashion during rituals of state.

SOLDIERS AND THROWSTICKS

Eminent scholars of Egyptian warfare have failed to agree on the use of the throwstick during the Predynastic Period. Although excavated remains are rare, throwsticks appear on predynastic stelae, inscribed funerary stones, and among hieroglyphic texts.

While there are no surviving material remains that can be dated to the Old Kingdom, it would be wrong to assume that the throwstick was without military function. In fact, it was probably in continuous use, which would explain the appearance of this weapon among battle scenes of the Middle Kingdom. Certainly, references to the function of the throwstick can be found in Old Kingdom texts and trading of throwsticks is known from the Archaic Period.

TWO

Middle Kingdom Warfare

A History of Middle Kingdom Warfare

The period of 160 years between the Old and Middle Kingdoms is known as the First Intermediate Period (2200-2040 BC). It covers the decline of the Old Kingdom, which eventually collapsed due to both economic crisis caused by the distribution of wealth and power among the nobles and, most probably, environmental factors that included an outbreak of famine. The transfer of power to the local rulers led to the development of private armies in several warring areas around Egypt.

Egypt erupted into violence. Trade broke down and Egypt was threatened by invaders from the east. During this time, several areas rose in importance, including Herakleopolis, a city that was regarded as an important strategic site, situated between the north and south of Egypt. The princes of Herakleopolis had enormous power and their reign remained uncontested until the rise of the house of Khety. Khety III began a feud with his southern neighbours the Thebans, who attempted to take control of the Herakleopolitan kingdom; the surrounding neighbours shifted their alliance between the two aggressors, often changing the conditions of their allegiance when it suited them. The conflict is described in the autobiography of Ankhtifi, a governer of Hierakonpolis.

> The general of Armant said to me. Come, worthy man, sail down to the fort of Armant. I then went down to the west of Armant, and I found that all the army of Thebes and Koptos had attacked the fort of Armant. I reached the west bank of Thebes. My brave, fine troops went to the west and the east of Thebes and prepared for battle. But none dared to come out of Thebes, for they were afraid. The whole of Upper Egypt died of hunger and each one had reached such a state of starvation that he ate his own children.

As described, the fighting took place around the area of Armant in Thebes. Ankhtifi's enemy was none other than one Inyotef I, the prince of Thebes.

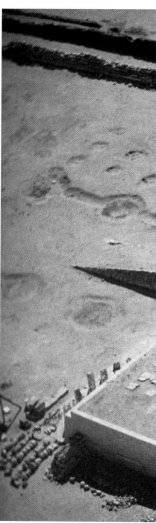

Fig. 29: A statue of Mentuhotpe II. *(Joann Fletcher/Egyptian Museum, Cairo)*

Inyotef gained control of southern Egypt, and conquered the nomes ruled by Hierakonpolis. His successor Inyotef II renewed the conflict. In middle Egypt the Thebans now made a desperate attempt to take the north.

Mentuhotpe II (Fig. 29) succeeded Inyotef in 2040 BC. A Theban prince who acted as the legitimate ruler of Egypt rather than as a provincial chief or governor, Mentuhotpe once again united the two kingdoms of Upper and Lower Egypt. He inherited the land from the first cataract in the south to the tenth nome of Upper Egypt – in between Mentuhotpe and the north lay the

Fig. 30: The ruined mortuary temple of Mentuhotpe II at Thebes. It is situated next to the temple of the New Kingdom ruler Hatshepsut and clearly influenced the design of the latter. *(Joann Fletcher/Deir el-Bahri, Thebes)*

town of Asyut which was still controlled by the provincial rulers. After much fighting Mentuhotpe captured Asyut, and ended a long period of internal struggles. He defeated the Herakleopolitan dynasty to become the founding ruler of the Middle Kingdom. Mentuhotpe was an excellent politician. He allowed the loyal governors of the allied provinces to keep their positions and retained Theban administrators in the area. Once again, trade and building projects flourished.

Mentuhotpe died after a reign of fifty-one years. His mortuary temple is built at Thebes and served as a prototype for the New Kingdom Temple of Queen Hatshepsut (Fig. 30). It also contained the burial chamber of a unique group of ancient Egyptian soldier mummies. These men, as we shall see later, are believed to have died in the war that brought about the reunification of Egypt and which resulted in the unifying rule of Mentuhotpe II.

The key provinces associated with the civil wars were el-Bersha, Asyut and Beni Hasan. While the tombs of each have produced an abundance of representations that show military themes, excavations conducted in these areas have also revealed objects of a military nature such as axes, bows and daggers. After a period of civil unrest, Mentuhotpe moved the capital of Egypt to Thebes; after his death his successors moved back to Memphis in the north. The Middle Kingdom is known as the classical age, when the calibre of Egyptian literature reached its peak. Wisdom texts, official literature and imaginative compositions are dated to this time. Texts from this period, namely, the Story of Sinuhe, The Shipwrecked Sailor and The Eloquent Peasant often contain themes of morality and justice, characteristics which played an important role in religious thought during the Middle Kingdom.

The Egyptian people had once relied on the king for their personal salvation. During the Middle Kingdom, the individual's survival in the afterlife came to require that he or she had lived a good and moral life. The cult of Osiris played a significant role in Middle Kingdom theology. His mystery plays were enacted every year at his cult centre at Abydos, and Osiris, the life-giver and god of fertility and regeneration, became a symbol of the victory of good over evil. After death, each person was expected to stand trial before Osiris, when their hearts were weighed against their deeds in the Hall of Judgment.

Few religious buildings have survived from this period, but one only has to look at the remains of the Temple of Mentuhotpe II at Deir el-Bahri, Thebes, to appreciate the elegant design and complexity of Middle Kingdom funerary complexes. Egyptian rulers built pyramid structures in the north at Dashur, el-Lisht and Hawara. During this period, too, new styles in royal statuary saw the development of mummiform figures while privately commissioned statues show officials in a state of prayer and block statues appear in the form of seated individuals whose legs are bent to the chin. These statues had large cuboid surfaces that were decorated with inscriptions.

The Egyptians had established control in the south where they set up a series of forts. Egypt also played a significant role in the politics of the Near East where countries such as Syria sealed their alliances with treasure or tribute.

During the Middle Kingdom Egypt also traded with Crete, and Minoan ceramics were found at Lahun and Abydos. Foreign workers came to Egypt, and large groups of Asiatics began to settle in the Delta. Under Sesostris I the Egyptians campaigned into Syria-Palestine. The Execrations Texts, magical figurines inscribed with the names of Egypt's enemies, were found in Nubia. The figures were ritually smashed and buried under buildings, just as the symbols of the 'Nine Bows', the traditional enemies of Egypt, were placed under the sandals of the king or on the floors of the royal palace.

SIEGE WARFARE

In the Middle East, acts of siege warfare can be traced back to the Neolithic Period. Excavations have uncovered fortified walls, some up to 34m thick, that were built in Mesopotamia around 3000 BC. However, the earliest evidence depicting fortified structures in Egypt is revealed in images carved in the form of clay models or archaic palettes and dates to the period around 3100 BC (Fig. 31).

When planning a siege, the topographical position of a citadel, its shape, size and its water source were primary concerns. The operation was designed to enable the offensive army to cover the perimeter of a citadel, and starve out the inhabitants by preventing supplies from reaching them. Once in position the army had to keep watch on every wall of the citadel, so that they could prevent the inhabitants from leaving the city to obtain help. In this respect, the offensive army became a vulnerable target, for if the latter became desperate, they would come under attack from the besieged inhabitants.

There are several methods used to breach a city wall. The soldiers could gain access from above the fort, or through its walls. The Egypt-

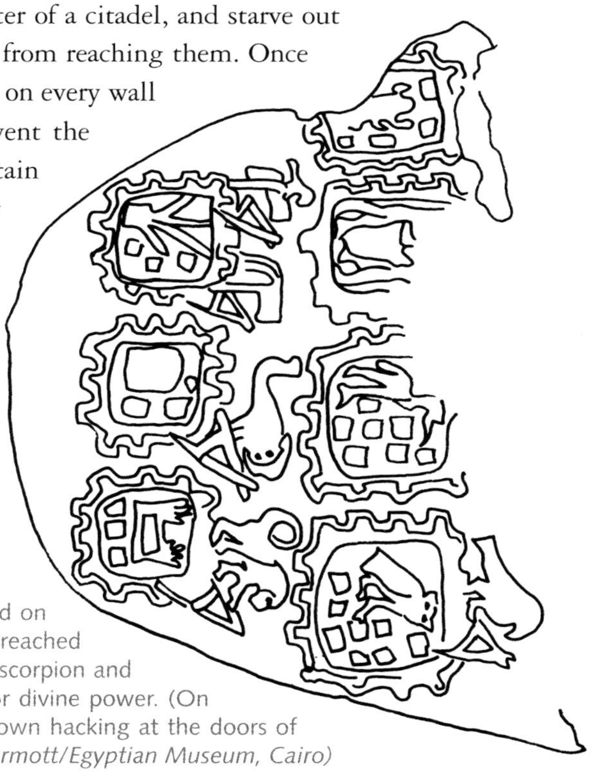

Fig. 31: A series of fortified cities is depicted on this archaic palette. Each citadel is being breached by a creature carrying a mattock. The lion, scorpion and falcon are emblems associated with royal or divine power. (On pages 140-1 New Kingdom soldiers are shown hacking at the doors of enemy strongholds, Fig. 89.) *(Bridget McDermott/Egyptian Museum, Cairo)*

ians used ladders to scale the perimeters. Ladders had to be engineered on the site of the siege, as they had to fit the specific wall measurements of forts; moreover, they were only effective on barriers less than 10m in height. In New Kingdom representations soldiers are shown cutting down the trees to be used for this purpose, while in scenes dating from the Middle Kingdom the Egyptians are often shown hacking away at city walls with axes or long narrow battering rams. This type of siege method, which can be seen on archaic palettes and in early tomb scenes, was used to break through the mud brick walls of enemy fortifications. Alternatively sappers could take the city from below, digging tunnels under the city walls, but there is no evidence that this method was employed in ancient Egypt. Many ancient tales of war reveal breaching by trickery and in ancient Egypt this concept was not unfamiliar. A text that dates to the New Kingdom reveals how the members of the Egyptian army gained access to an enemy stronghold in the city of Joppa by hiding their soldiers in baskets that were to be transported into the city complex.

Siege warfare demanded a great deal of time and manpower; it required the Egyptians to make complex mathematical calculations and use sophisticated engineering techniques. Although archaeologists have learned a great deal about these practices from Assyrian sources, little evidence of Egyptian military logistics has survived. Written evidence, dating to the New Kingdom, suggests that operations of this kind could last over long periods: in one instance, the army of Tuthmosis III lay siege to Megiddo for seven months. During this period, the Egyptians were faced with problems that commonly resulted from operations of this type. Long-term occupation of a site would have induced certain psychological reactions since occupation was essentially a waiting game and the army would have faced issues such as boredom and decling morale. Equally, they were vulnerable to surprise attacks from the enemy. And there were other hazards. A series of medical complaints and diseases could arise among units of men encamped over a long period – these would include lice infestations, dysentery and infections of the feet. Moreover, the process itself was expensive, and the Egyptians had to make use of the surrounding natural resources to provide food, warmth and shelter.

A HISTORY OF FORTIFICATION

Fortified structures are known in Egypt from the Predynastic Period (3150 BC). During the Old Kingdom (2700–2190 BC) the Egyptians built protective structures in the southern regions; these included a defensive wall known as 'swn' (*soon*) which may have given the area its modern name, Aswan. The first cataract acted as an impenetrable barrier to shipping; at this point boats had to be lifted out of the water and transported along the river bank before they could continue their journey. During the New Kingdom the Egyptians built defensive walls and citadels along the western desert, Sinai and the Mediterranean coast. They also maintained a chain of fortified buildings in the south. During the reign of Amenemhat I, the eastern delta was lined with a series of forts known as the 'walls of the prince', which were designed to protect Egypt against invasion from the Levant.

A common royal epithet of the period includes the phrase that revealed the king's intention to 'extend the borders of Egypt', a term that refers to the Egyptian programme of expansion and domination. In order to retain their control of foreign conquests, the Egyptians built fort stations that enabled them to monitor shipping and trading caravans, as well as defend their territory. During the Middle Kingdom copper and gold mines were exploited and became important assets to the Egyptian economy. The forts were designed to enhance and protect the Egyptians and their interests in Nubia; in this respect they were placed at the points where trading routes left the river. Donkey caravans were used to transport food and water to the mines. We have no records of garrisons being besieged, however, excavations have shown that fires were common. These may have been due to metalworking processes that were employed at the sites.

While forts were constructed with mud brick, timber was employed above the door frames, and stone was used for paving. A system of towers was built around the fort, along with an overhanging platform. When the fort was attacked, stones could be thrown from the parapet or dropped through traps along the floor. Towers were set at intervals along the structure at no more than 30m apart; this meant that no 'dead' space occurred between them, and that soldiers were able to fire in two directions. The battlement was usually designed with a crenellated parapet which covered the surface of the walls which were themselves designed with merlons and embrasures through which the archers or stone throwers would fire their weapons. The Egyptian forts shared similar plans, which included workshops, barracks, officers' quarters and a temple. The inner area of the fort was lined with streets and drains. Most were linked to the Nile by a covered passageway. Each fort was given a title such as 'Warding off the Bows', a direct reference to the Egyptian term used for the traditional enemies of Egypt, who were known as 'the Nine Bows'.

Buhen

The fortress of Buhen was situated at the northern end of the second cataract. At first Buhen was little more than a walled settlement, but during the Middle Kingdom the Egyptians embarked on a large-scale military expansion into Nubia, and reinforced the station until it became a complex citadel, with its own stores, temples and permanent army.

Buhen was just one of a series of Middle Kingdom forts that were built over a period of 130 years, between the reigns of Sesostris I and Sesostris III. The Egyptians built these structures from mud brick, a common component in the construction of ancient Egyptian buildings; the bricks were formed from the alluvial mud of the Nile and were often mixed with chaff. The bricks were left to dry on mats or in moulds outside in the sun. The bricks used in the construction of Middle Kingdom forts were much larger than those used in the average Egyptian dwelling. The Egyptians solved the problem of drying large bricks and avoiding longitudinal cracking by placing dried grass at regular intervals along the layers. Once dry, the completed walls would have been covered with plaster and decorated with military insignia.

The fortress of Buhen was built and designed with a rectangular outer structure. The outer enclosure of the building measured 700m in length and was 4m thick; a ditch was constructed around the outside of the walls. The wall was strengthened at intervals by 32 bastions. The western wall was designed with a large tower which eventually rose 47m in height. It had double wooden doors and a drawbridge that was activated by rollers. The wall was also built with five smaller towers. The inner walls of the fort were 5m thick and at least 11m high, they were provided with corner towers and bastions set at 5m

Fig. 32: There was a fort at Buhen as early as the Old Kingdom. This complex Middle Kingdom structure was designed with bastions, a glacis and a drawbridge that was activated by rollers. *(E.E.S. Archives)*

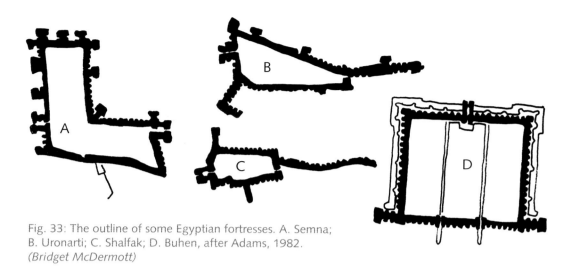

Fig. 33: The outline of some Egyptian fortresses. A. Semna;
B. Uronarti; C. Shalfak; D. Buhen, after Adams, 1982.
(Bridget McDermott)

intervals, each having a series of small loop holes that provided space for the
archers or sling men to attack the enemy below.

Forts that were built at a later date show an attempt to improve on the
Buhen design (Fig. 33). For example, the fort of Kuban reveals several modified
features. Here, the Egyptians had attempted to widen the defence line and
ditch. Equally, the fortress of Mirgissa was elevated to a cliff top, while the
Semna fort, an L-shaped enclosure, covered the level area of a steep rocky hill.
The fort of Uronarti was constructed on an island; it was triangular in shape,
and fortified by a series of sloping walls designed with bastions. The fortress of
Askut also lay on an island in the Batn el-Hajar, just south of the second
cataract. While the other Nubian forts were built in clusters, Askut was
situated in a desolate area close to a gold mining site. However, the fort could
accommodate a large population; excavations have shown that it had an
enormous storage area, which covered almost half of the citadel. Because of this,
scholars have suggested that the granary at Askut would have housed the main
rations supply that would sustain a large percentage of the Egyptian soldiers in
the Nubian region. It is estimated that the stores were capable of supplying the
food for 5,628 people per year.

THE SOLDIERS OF KING MENTUHOTPE II

During the season of 1925/6 Herbert Winlock, employed by the Metropolitan
Museum of Art expedition, was working on the west bank at Luxor, ancient
Thebes, in an area located close to the Valley of the Kings. Winlock was

particularly interested in the history of the 11th Dynasty. During the early 1920s he spent a great deal of time examining the remains uncovered in the area around the temple of Mentuhotpe II at Deir el-Bahri. He found and entered some catacombs directly below the temple wall; he discovered that each had a corridor which had been lengthened as extra burials had been included. The tomb was lower than those of the great nobles, and had been buried by a rock fall from the cliff face almost 35m above. In one of the tombs Winlock found sixty mummies. Although it is possible that the bodies had originally been kept in coffins – for small fragments of wood were found in the vicinity of the corpses – they were discovered stacked together and wrapped in bandages. The bodies had probably been dried in sand after they were recovered from the battlefield, and no other embalming chemicals were evident. Winlock believed that the bodies were the remains of military leaders who had been given an honourable burial close to their king.

Winlock described the contents as a 'gruesome' discovery, and referred to the stench and the decayed state of the bodies as they were taken out into the hot sun. At first the bodies reminded him of those of Coptic Christian monks. At a time when the world was still reeling from the amazing discoveries from the tomb of Tutankhamun, Winlock felt disappointed with his discovery, and resealed the tomb, which remained closed for the next three years. In 1926 the contents were once more examined, and the excavators found a large collection of bandages or shrouds that were marked with hieroglyphic symbols. Winlock offered a small reward to the Egyptian workers for every marked fragment they could find, and eventually he was able to recover over sixty samples of cloth that were printed with the names of the soldiers; for example, the names of Sobekhotep and Senwosret were clearly identified.

Dr Douglas E. Derry, professor of anatomy at the Kasr el-Ainy Medical School in Cairo, examined the bodies after they had been placed in a makeshift tent outside the tomb. While conducting his examination on the tenth body Derry's attention was caught by an object protruding from the soldier's chest cavity. The remains of an arrow. As the archaeologists re-examined the bodies they found many arrow wounds that were now evident when they looked more closely at the dried skin of the men. They realised that they had found the tomb of a group of soldiers. The men had been buried in a catacomb that would usually have been reserved for members of the royal household. After several examinations it was found that the soldiers had been placed in the tomb before it had been finished, for the tools of the tomb cutters were found inside the burial chamber. The tomb was less than 1m high.

The Soldiers

Derry estimated the average height of the men to have been 1.68m – a good height for an Egyptian male. However, Winlock identified the bodies as those of a Nubian race, for their hair resembled that of the Nubian peoples depicted on Egyptian monuments. Some of the soldiers bore old scars, so it is possible that some of the men were veteran warriors. The men had suffered a great many injuries to the skull and face. Winlock tried to estimate the age of the soldiers; he came to the conclusion that they were between the ages of thirty and forty as their teeth were in a serious state of decay and three men were seen to have grey hair. However, it is important to note that grey hair and tooth decay are common among Egyptian males under the age of thirty.

The hair of the soldiers was cut short, some of the locks had been twisted so that the thick tresses would provide some form of protection for the head. Two of the soldiers had beards. Although these soldiers were identified as archers, only fragments of weapons were found with the bodies; but the remains of wristguards were still attached to the limbs, while other examples were found lying among the tomb debris. The excavators found the remains of a bow tip, its twisted gut bow cord still attached; they also came across a plaited linen cord, which would have been used as a bowstring.

It was surmised that six of the bodies had been attacked by carrion birds as there was evidence of shredded flesh found on several of the bodies, indicating that the men had been left on the battlefield for some time. Arrow tips were also found among the soldiers' hair; some had produced small wounds although the larger gashes found on the skulls were caused by missiles that had been thrown from above the soldiers' heads during battle. Examples of arrow wounds include that of a gash 25mm long found on the upper arm of a soldier, while a wooden arrow tip 70mm long was discovered between the rib cartilages and the skin of another. The remaining fragment was curved across the sternum while the root remained in the neck. In another soldier, an arrow had entered the left side of the body between the ribs at the inferior angle of the scapula, its velocity sufficient to send it directly across the chest cavity where it became fixed in both the left lung and the heart. Other arrows were found in the auxillary space below a small round hole at the base of the neck of yet another soldier, with clear evidence of a haemorrhage around the wound. The arrow was shown to have crossed the bottom of the left eye socket and penetrated the back of the nose and the head. Other men were found to have wounds where the arrow tips remained in place; one was found in the right scapula, and it was clear that it had hit the soldier as he lay wounded on the ground. Some soldiers had wounds that clearly demonstrated that the arrow had penetrated the lungs and the ribs. Here there is often evidence of extensive bleeding in the left side of the chest. One soldier had arrow fragments lodged in the hair, but they had created no scalp wounds. Three fragments of arrow tips, along with body tissue, were found among the debris of bandages and bodies in the tomb. Another soldier had a puncture wound on the left side of the skull, the bone was depressed in two fragments which still adhered to the inner side of the cranial cavity. This wound may have resulted from an arrow striking the soldier's head with enormous force; indeed, Middle Kingdom military scenes often depict images of the enemy brought down by arrows in this way.

The Battle Scene

Examination of the remains indicated that the wounds described above were caused by arrows or sling stones that were thrown from a precipice – perhaps from the wall of a fort or a ridge high above a plain where the soldiers were trapped. During the battle, the soldiers of Mentuhotpe were beaten back and the offensive army was able to return to the battlefield where they finished off the wounded either by stabbing or smashing their heads with blunt instruments, probably staves or mace; examination certainly shows that the soldiers had suffered a high percentage of head wounds and broken noses. Some wounds were inflicted postmortem and it is evident that soldiers were making sure their enemies were truly dead. Blood stains were common, and it is clear that many of the soldiers lay bleeding to death on the field. Cuts and blows were administered with massive force. At some point the attackers retreated and the bodies were attacked by carrion birds. The skin and muscle from the legs, knees and feet had been shredded, as had the arms, arteries and tendons. The abdomen and chest of one individual had suffered much damage. All the bodies had been coated with sand and dried before bandaging; the bodies had been naturally desiccated with the hands placed by the sides and the legs extended. Some were found with ankles crossed, the forearms flexed with the hands hooked over the shoulders or placed under the right side of the face. There were no signs of embalming – the nails, toes and fingers were present, and tendons were well preserved. While the internal organs were recognisable, the genitals had become bloated during the putrefaction process. Sand was found on the bodies and in the thickly matted hair. The wounds were covered with sand, which was also found in the eyes and mouth; sand had been rubbed into the wounds and placed inside the skulls. The men were wrapped in linen bandages while still on the battlefield; several layers of sheet linen had been placed on each body.

SOLDIERS AND ARMOUR

Middle Kingdom

Head Protection
Although examinations conducted on the remains of the mercenary soldiers of Mentuhotpe II reveal the fact that hair extensions were used to protect the skulls of ancient warriors from arrowheads, there is no evidence to suggest that the Egyptian soldier employed metallic or fabric head protection until the New Kingdom.

Breast Armour
During the Middle Kingdom soldiers adopted a series of leather straps, which were worn crossed and fitted around the shoulders. This type of garment, also worn by sailors, dancers and acrobats, was used as a grip, as an attachment device and as a light form of protection to deflect arrows and shield the breast from blows. Soldiers from this period also wore abdominal bodices secured by shoulder straps worn over the front of the body and attached around the neck and waist by thongs, which were probably made of padded linen. The importance of this garment is highlighted by its adoption by the god Horus of Buhen during the 12th Dynasty, suggesting that this type of bodice had become a major feature of military iconography. It was known as a *qny* (keny). Finally, it is the tomb paintings of el-Bersha that reveal the first example of the true breastplate: soldiers are shown with panels of leather or reinforced linen inserted within the breast straps to protect the centre of the chest (Figs 34 and 55).

Fig. 34: These Middle Kingdom soldiers, taken from tomb paintings at el-Bersha, are armed with a splayed axe, a large body shield, a long spear and a javelin. (*Bridget McDermott*)

Shields

During this period the Egyptian army utilised a range of body shields that were often depicted on tomb walls, coffin panels and on the canopy of model boats. The soldiers adopted three types of shield. While a light buckler about 1m in height was commonly used by infantry, a full-length shield was also displayed in the tombs of Asyut. The grips used on the inside of these shields can measure several metres in length (Figs 34 and 55). However, the most unique and striking development of this period was a massive siege shield shown in battle scenes from the tombs at Beni Hasan. The sheer size of these shields meant that several soldiers were needed to operate them. In this way it may have debilitated military manoeuvres and it was quickly abandoned by the time of the late Middle Kingdom.

SOLDIERS AND ARCHERY

Bows

Although weapons were issued from the state, archers were responsible for the maintenance of their own equipment which was distributed from stores of the type shown in scenes from the tomb of Senbi at Meir. It is probable that archers carried their own kitbags (Fig. 35); one surviving example of this type of bag

Fig. 35: The only surviving example of an archer's kitbag. His wristguards and bowstrings can clearly be seen, while a pot and samples of malachite were also found in the bag. *(Bridget McDermott/Metropolitan Museum of Art)*

Fig. 36: Here an archer uses his knee to secure his bow while he re-strings the weapon. From Beni Hasan. Tomb 15. Tomb of Baqt III. *(Bridget McDermott)*

contained spare strings, a wrist guard, and polishing stones. Lumps of malachite were also included in the archers' kit, their probable purpose being to aid vision and protect the eyes.

Contacts with the outside world, especially those with Assyria, led to the crafting of advanced weaponry. However, both the double convex bow and the self-bow survived as military weapons. A bow from the tomb of Antefoker is clearly designed with a compound construction. Simple bows from Senebtisi's tomb were cut from natural branches and remained unpainted, with both limb ends protected with gold capsules.

Bows of the double convex type appear during the Middle Kingdom Period. In the tomb of Achtoy, a large curved bow was found which functioned as both a hunting and military weapon. Although depictions from the tomb of Senbi illustrate the hunting tradition, two types of bow were shown in storage, with the strung bows shown in duplicate. A pair of curved bows was depicted with concave bellies and rounded limbs, while the others were identified as plain bows and were shown among hieroglyphic signs in both strung and unstrung conditions.

While gut strings were used in conjunction with Middle Kingdom bows, strips of linen, which proved more efficient than the former, were also used. Several gut bowstrings of the 11th Dynasty have been examined and pieces of twisted gut 240mm in length and 2mm thick are discussed in an analytical study of the remains found in the tomb of the soldiers of Mentuhotpe. Often, gut was discovered attached to broken bow ends. Bowstrings were usually fitted just before military engagement, when the line was looped over one end of the upright limb which was then bent by the weight of the soldier's body so that

Fig. 37: A collection of various Middle Kingdom bows and arrows in the British Museum collection. To the right of the weapons a wooden bow box can be seen. *(Bridget McDermott/British Museum Collection)*

the string could be affixed to the foot; alternatively, the kneeling archer would grip the bow between his knees and stretch the string vertically across his bow (Fig. 36). Among the remains of the mummies identified as the archers of Mentuhotpe there is evidence to indicate that the bowstring was attached by being laid along the shaft where it was secured to the bow limbs by a system of eleven loops or twists. When these twists were wound around the cord, the cord was tightened, pulling the limbs of the bow into a gradual state of tension. It would be logical to assume that the archer would carry spare bowstrings since they would often snap on application and need to be swiftly replaced; although there is no evidence of this practice, spare bowstrings have been discovered in the kitbag of an archer, and may have been worn around the head.

The remains of Middle Kingdom bows have also been recovered among ancient tomb equipment found in the vicinity of the Temple of Mentuhotpe at Thebes,

Detail of the wooden bow box on p. 55. (*Bridget McDermott/British Museum Collection*)

while others were found among the contents of a 12th Dynasty priest burial. Bows were known, too, to have been included among the burial equipment of women while dummy models were also included amidst funerary equipment, and a replica armoury found in the tomb of Nakht at Asyut also included two bows.

Bowmen were employed by mourners during Middle Kingdom funerals. Their importance within the context of funerary ritual is evident in literary tales of the period, such as the 'Story of Sinuhe': 'It is no small matter that your corpse will be interred without being escorted by bowmen.' At the end of the Middle Kingdom and the beginning of the New Kingdom, bows were often placed within coffins. Bows were frequently dismembered, or 'killed' as a ritualistic practice during funerals and there is evidence to suggest that archery equipment was designed with such ritual breaking in mind. Broken bows that are dated to this period have frequently been recovered. For instance, a bow, which had been deliberately sawn in two pieces was recovered from a site at Saqqara where it was not uncommon to find archery equipment placed in close proximity to the deceased. This practice appears to have accelerated during the Middle Kingdom, giving substance to the belief that every Theban of the 11th Dynasty retained his bow beside him in death. Some nobles did indeed maintain a large armoury and wished to depict themselves upon stelae with their bows (Fig. 38). The ritualistic practice of the breaking of the bow had numerous connotations. As a symbolic act it may have implied the breaking of the enemy spirit, a common belief still held among warriors of North Africa, or it may have symbolised the metaphorical separation of the spirit from the body – the arrow released from the bow. In the story of Sinuhe, this point is clearly emphasised in the words, 'Slacken your bow, lay down your arrow' – a phrase that is associated with the physical death of the body.

Although shells were found attached to the wristguards of the archers of Mentuhotpe there is, surprisingly, no artistic evidence to show the use of amulets among the military, a practice that is otherwise universally found throughout the history of warfare. However, the use of shells by Nubian archers can be compared with practices adopted by modern Sudanese tribesmen who still wear shells as protective charms. Some shells are pierced with small holes that are capable of producing audible signals. The absence of amuletic decoration among representations of ancient Egyptian soldiers is surprising, although numerous scenes show men wearing feathers in their hair. Although this custom was not unique to the archery corps, the feather had an obvious connection to bowmen, and there is some literary evidence to suggest that the feather was used as an amulet. For instance, in the Edwin Smith Papyrus there are references to the protective forces that the feather could procure: 'Speak the word over the vulture feather, with which a man has covered himself, placed as his protection in every place he goes. It is a protection against the year expelling sickness in the year of the pest.' The work of vultures, evident upon the desecrated bodies of fallen soldiers, highlights the deepest fears of the Egyptians regarding their mortality and physical preservation. The use of the vulture feather was probably intended to serve as an amulet. The feather was also associated with Ma'at, the manifestation of chaos conquered.

Aside from their military and ritualistic functions, bows also appear in other contexts. Commemorative objects were often marked with the depiction of their owner's archery equipment, a practice which attests to the special status of the archer among soldiers of the Egyptian army. Officials were often portrayed with their bows on funerary stelae of this period, where they are shown clutching the bow in one hand and a sheaf of arrows in the other (Fig. 38). The term 'strong of arm' is often used to refer to the prowess of the archer. Soldiers are traditionally

shown with two bows, a dualistic theme also demonstrated on coffin panels where bows are usually depicted in pairs. A curved bow was shown as part of the interior decor of the 12th Dynasty coffin of the estate manager Achtoy from el-Lisht. These bows, which are always curved, are shown both with and without a protective wrapping. A fragmentary scene from the tomb of Amenemhat depicts an archer carrying two simple bows that were protected by limb guards. Another example of this practice can be identified in a processional scene from the tomb of Khety.

Model archers, crafted in wood, were used to exemplify companies of land soldiers. The most famous and well preserved of these objects is the model of the soldiers of Meserheti in Cairo Museum (Fig. 39) that depicts forty archers armed with the traditional self-bow. A model archer armed with a broken bow can also be seen in the Museum of Fine Arts, Boston. Similarly, in their capacity as river sentries, archers are depicted on model boats (Fig. 40). They are often shown with tools and weapons tucked in their kilts. Additionally, the figure of a bowman appears on a boat among examples of Middle Kingdom rock graffiti.

Archers were shown with more frequency than any other group of soldiers in the tombs of Beni Hasan and often served as a protective screen for the siege charge. They were also depicted in minor roles, recovering arrows from the dead. It seems that soldiers repossessed their arrows after battle, including weapons that had struck or injured the enemy, a practice that is clearly illustrated in the tomb of Baqt III at Beni Hasan. Here, scenes portray the various stages the archer adopted in stringing and shooting the bow. In most instances, archers are depicted clasping three arrows. At Beni Hasan, the attempt to distinguish military figures was achieved by placing figures of pale and dark skinned soldiers in juxtaposition – while the pale bowmen carry auxiliary weapons, the darker figures are shown with arrow sheaths. It is, however, impossible to distinguish the rank of the soldiers shown in these representations.

Traditionally bowmen were associated with dogs, animals that played a vital role in scouting and reconnaissance. The role of the master of the kennels is known from the fortress at Buhen, and elaborate canine collars have been retrieved from important burial sites including that of Tutankhamun. Bowmen employed as royal bodyguards in military displays were often depicted with these animals.

Opposite: Fig. 38: The stele of a bowman and his dog. The bowman is shown in a traditional pose with his bow in one hand and a sheaf of arrows in the other. *(Bridget McDermott/Museo Archeologico, Florence)*

In the Middle Kingdom, archers are often portrayed within a sophisticated narrative structure, and bowmen are shown inspecting groups of corpses which lie on the battlefield (Fig. 41). The retrieval of battle casualties is exemplified in the case of the soldiers of Mentuhotpe, who were brought back to Egypt with their bodies covered and protected by sand. Although this event is often referred to as a unique act of respect, it is possible that other soldiers were also able to bring back their dead in this manner.

Fig. 39: The Meserheti model archers. This model shows forty archers placed on a pedestal of wood, marching in rows of four. They hold their bows in one hand, their arrows in the other. *(Bridget McDermott/Egyptian Museum, Cairo)*

Bowmen were shown in the tomb of Khety, where they are presented as part of a military procession marching before the king. Archers were frequently shown as bodyguards and incorporated among the Middle Kingdom processional ranks. Two archers who appear in the same funerary chamber can be identified in a military procession which marched behind the tomb owner Tjeuti-Hetep. The soldiers press their bows against their chests, demonstrating the Middle Kingdom military salute. In paintings from the tomb of

Fig. 40: Soldiers who manned model boats of the Middle Kingdom are often shown with tools and weapons tucked into the back of their kilts. Military ships often displayed large shields, which were attached to, or painted on to, the boat's canopy. *(Bridget McDermott/ Ashmolean Museum, Oxford)*

Amenemhat, bowmen are illustrated in several ways. Soldiers are shown before a fortress battlement, their arrows placed upright, in readiness to shoot. The archers are protected by shield-bearers, and in their turn protect the soldiers who lay siege to the fort with a battering ram. Two archers from this tomb are shown on the fort precipice, with their bow-lines extended. Bowmen in this tomb are shown flanked by axe and javelin men, while one individual is depicted actually firing arrows at the enemy.

Although it is clear that these units were engaged in well-practised and calculated drills, single archers are often shown running randomly behind the troops holding sheaths above their heads and it is possible that these men were responsible for issuing fresh supplies. It is evident that the army used

Fig. 41: In this scene from Tomb 15, the Tomb of Baqt III, at Beni Hasan, enemy soldiers are shown with neck wounds. Egyptian arrows were propelled with limited force, and soldiers were more likely to die of infection from arrow wounds rather than from the impact itself. In this way, the Egyptian bowmen must have been trained to aim their arrows at the most vulnerable part of the body, the neck. *(Bridget McDermott)*

Fig. 55: These three Middle Kingdom soldiers from Tomb 2, the Tomb of Tehuti-Hetep at El Bersha, are carrying a typical large body shield, a splayed axe and a spear. The soldier on the left wears a breast plate beneath the straps across his chest. *(Bridget McDermott)*

alternating formations of archers and spearmen during combat. Archers armed with a lightweight bow operated beside spearmen and provided a potent force against an army that relied on infantrymen alone. Archers could hold their ground, safely out of missile range, allowing their spearmen to advance against the enemy under a hail of covering fire. It has been suggested that the Middle Kingdom bow had a range of between 50 and 60m, which may be compared with the modern Sudanese bow that has a firing range of 87.5m. In combat, archers were used to soften up enemy formations, a practice that can be seen in artistic representations where archers are always depicted at the forefront of military action. This position may exemplify the special status that archers retained among the army corps.

Arrows

During the First Intermediate Period, evidence for military weapons is non-existent, and we must refrain from interpretation during this phase. Certainly, the Egyptians were still manufacturing barbed arrowheads (Fig. 42), which can be identified in hieroglyphic texts. Many examples of 6th Dynasty bows were recovered from the site of Asyut. However, there are no representational sequences among known Third Intermediate Period pictorial art.

Traditionally, Egyptian arrows were made of reed and wood. The foreshaft, which was slightly tapered and rounded, formed a tang that was often inserted into reed (Fig. 43). The junction was layered by a binding of sinew or thread, and thickly covered with black mastic. Fletching methods have rarely been discussed.

Fig. 42: A fine example of a barbed flint arrowhead dated to the Middle Kingdom. *(Bridget McDermott/British Museum Collection)*

Fig. 43: The foreshaft of this arrow forms a tang that was inserted into the reed and sealed with mastic. On impact the arrow snapped away, leaving the arrowhead firmly fixed in the target. *(Bridget McDermott/British Museum Collection)*

Fig. 44: A rare example of this ancient fletching technique can be seen on this Middle Kingdom arrow. *(Bridget McDermott/British Museum Collection)*

However, this type of craftsmanship can be identified among arrows of modern African tribes, where point sections of arrowheads are inserted into arrow-shafts so that the piece detaches once the arrow finds its mark. This prevents the arrowhead from being drawn out by the weight of the shaft on impact, and prevents the arrow from snapping. Arrows could be crafted to a meter in length, although generally they vary from 559 to 864mm. There are many anomalies in calculations of the length of Middle Kingdom arrows, and it is impossible in the context of this study to attempt a definitive analysis of these measurements. Arrows were frequently tipped with a multi-barb or triangular metal head. They were fletched with three feathers and glued along the arrow-shaft at equal distances (Fig. 44). Other arrowheads were constructed from flint and secured by a firm black paste (Fig. 45). Although flint was still commonly used in the manufacture of arrowheads wood and ebony have also been found with lateral barbs. Arrowheads, crafted with barbs, enabled the weapon to fix rigidly in flesh. Two arrowheads are generally classed as hunting types: the transverse nock and the rounded barb, both of which are identified in military scenes. The archers

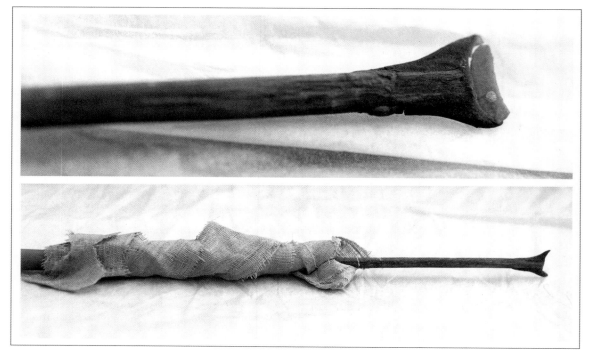

Fig. 45: These arrows from Asyut can be dated to the 6th Dynasty. The shaft is made of reed and the arrowhead is fixed with mastic, on which a transverse arrowhead of flint is placed. Another arrow of the transverse type was found wrapped in linen. *(Bridget McDermott/British Museum Collection)*

Fig. 46: This 6th Dynasty arrow was designed with a long wooden head. It was crafted to stun the target rather than pierce it. Although this type has been found with military arrows, its function on the battlefield is unclear. *(Bridget McDermott/British Museum Collection)*

depicted on the Meserheti model also carry arrows of this class. Arrows crafted with long straight heads are shown in the tomb of Senbi (Fig. 46) and together with splayed arrows were used for hunting purposes.

When Winlock examined the bodies of Mentuhotpe's soldiers, he found that ten men had been wounded or killed by ebony-tipped reed arrows; an example of the latter was found in the hair of a mummified soldier. Three fragments were found with the material remains discovered among the bodies of the slain soldiers of Mentuhotpe. Arrowheads of copper are also known from this period. The advantage of this metal lay in the fact that it was hard enough to produce a sharp penetrating point, but soft enough to buckle against bone. Copper therefore provided a more efficient warhead in comparison with materials such as wood and bone and the manufacture of copper arrowheads is mentioned in Middle Kingdom texts. The earliest metal arrowhead recovered in Egypt was found in a sandbed at Saqqara, and is dated to the 2nd Dynasty.

Bows and arrows of the Middle Kingdom were often found interred together in graves while the ritualistic 'killing' of bows and arrows continued throughout the New Kingdom Period. A group of arrows was found in the tomb of Sebekhetep while large groups of arrows, with individual arrows measuring up to a metre in length, were also found at Thebes and el-Lisht, together with two strung bows. Sixty arrows dating from the Middle Kingdom were recovered with bows; they were discovered in groups of five and eighteen, together with long reed arrows with hard wooden points.

During the Middle Kingdom, weapons were regarded as possessing religious and mythical identities and representations of gods and goddesses were armed with archery equipment, the bow having now become a fundamental object of ancient Egyptian ceremony. Arrows were also adopted and worn as protective amulets.

The use of painted arrow tips is well documented as a practice associated with the administration of poison or menstrual blood, intended to deliver death or infertility to the enemy. Today, poisoned arrows are still commonly crafted in tribal cultures, with the poison usually derived from scorpion or snake venom. Although it is impossible to identify traces of this type of poison on ancient artefacts, it is important to recognise that this type of secretion was available and well known to the ancient Egyptians. The addition of pigmentation marks may have provided a method of identification, either to enable the soldier to retrieve his own arrows, or to define the number of enemies he had injured or killed.

Arrows can also be identified in a manufacturing scene from the tomb of Amenemhat at Beni Hasan. Here they are depicted in dark grey pigment and are shown striped, with barbed wings. Archers are also depicted in shooting positions in the tombs located in this area, and rare scenes depict groups of arrows in motion (Fig. 47). The arrows are dispatched in both directions between the Egyptian and the enemy soldiers. This scene is a rare illustration of vulnerable Egyptian soldiers caught under siege, an image that creates a sense of danger and uncertain destiny rarely seen within the canon of Egyptian art.

Arrows can be seen, too, clutched in the hands of archers on two Middle Kingdom fragments. An enemy soldier, pierced with arrows, is represented on another fragment from the same collection, where the legs and breast are emphasised as vulnerable areas. Transverse arrow heads are illustrated in the tomb of Senbi at Meir; they are also carried by the Meserheti soldiers. The straight-tipped arrowhead is evident in scenes from the tomb of Senbi, and it is clear that both types were used in human combat. Here the archer, clasping three arrows, is shown extending his bow to the limit.

Fig. 47: Egyptian artists rarely depicted the dispatching of arrows. This unique scene from Tomb 2 at Beni Hasan reveals arrows in motion. *(Bridget McDermott)*

In scenes from Beni Hasan, we find images of the dead or injured struck by arrows with the most frequent injuries illustrated being neck wounds. In one scene arrows can clearly be seen protruding from the neck of an enemy soldier (Fig. 41). A complementary scene appears in narrative form during a description of Sinuhe's duel, when an arrow was shot into the neck of the champion of Retinu.

> He came to where I was, having approached him. Every heart was on fire for me, the women cried. All hearts ached for me, thinking 'Is there another who could fight him?' He raised up his axe and shield, while his arm of javelins fell towards me. When I had let his weapons attack, I let his arrows pass by me without a care, one passed by with the other. Then, when he charged at me, I shot him, my arrow fixed into his neck. He screamed and fell on his nose; I dispatched him with his axe. I made a war cry over him, and every Asiatic cried out. I gave praise to Montu, and his people mourned.

Note that in this instance the neck wound was not fatal, the injured party being finally dispatched by Sinuhe's axe. However, to the Egyptian archer the neck must have seemed the most vulnerable part of the body; indeed images of neck wounds are common in battle scenes.

Although a light contingent of men were used as runners, to supply and retrieve javelins and arrows, archers carried their own kitbags, and were responsible for sharpening and protecting their weapons. The contents of the kitbag included pebbles for the sharpening or polishing of arrowheads, an operation described in the story of Sinuhe: 'I strung my bow, sorted my arrows, practised with my dagger, polished my weapons.'

Arrowheads recovered from the Beni Hasan site were also protected by linen wrappings (Fig. 48), and it seems that individual arrows were wrapped in this manner during transport and storage.

Quivers

Quivers were used during the Middle Kingdom for the transportation of weapons such as arrows, staves, spears and javelins. Large quivers, adapted for carrying staves, are commonly depicted during this period, and are invariably shown crafted from stitched panels of black and white bovine hide. Artistic images show soldiers bearing quivers upon their shoulders, as if to emphasise their weight. A scene from Beni Hasan reveals the contents of a quiver to be long curved batons that can be compared with archers' quivers from the same

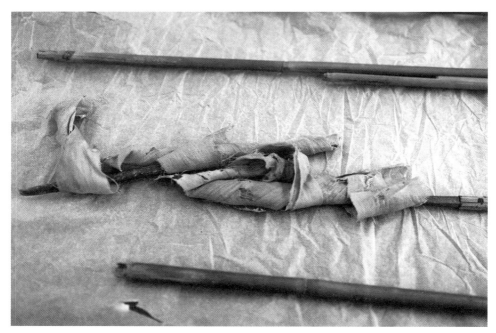

Above and below: Fig. 48: Arrows were wrapped in thin strips of linen to prevent damage. They were discovered in this state in bow boxes and quivers dated to the Middle Kingdom. *(Bridget McDermott/British Museum Collection)*

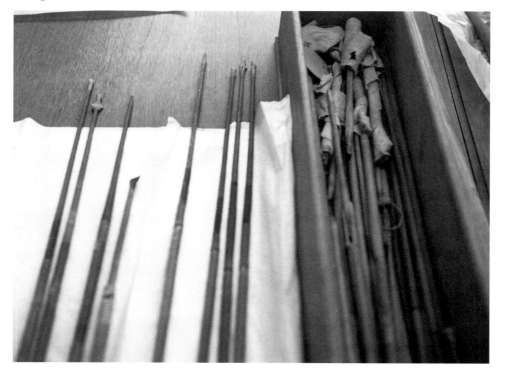

scene. Material remains of quivers from this period provide fine examples of leather craft; however, quivers were also woven in reed. A basketwork quiver recovered from a tomb of the 11th Dynasty at Thebes and found in close proximity to a group of model arrows, measured 114mm in diameter and 635mm in length. A parallel example is displayed in the Rijksmuseum van Oudheden, Leiden. Arrows were also transported in wooden cases (Fig. 49), which were secured by sliding panels and wooden pegs; these objects were probably used to transport weapons to the battlefield.

Variations in the design of the quiver were emphasised within the canon of Middle Kingdom military art. For example, quivers crafted from natural fibres had elongated caps and were often associated with land soldiers. They were included among the regalia of those soldiers engaged in military processions, and were carried by members of the bodyguard of Tjeuti-Hetep and Senbi in their tomb depictions at el-Bersha. The lid of the quiver was decorated in striped bands, and the arrows were placed upright inside the case.

Fig. 49: This wooden case is decorated with hunting scenes. It would contain large groups of arrows. It was closed by means of a wooden lid that could slide into place and was secured with wooden pegs. This type of case would have been used to transport weapons; it would not have been employed on the field. *(Bridget McDermott/British Museum Collection)*

A unique wooden model from the 11th Dynasty site of el-Bersha depicts a group of eight marching soldiers, three of whom carry large bow cases which were painted to imitate hide. From the same tomb, another wooden model represents soldiers carrying quivers that were pegged to their arms. The soldiers lean their quivers against the shoulder and the cases measure the complete arm span. One quiver is decorated with a white zigzag pattern, while the second is painted in black and white spots. Large quivers, which were designed to hold javelins or spears, were often carried in this manner. Large quivers that were attached to the canopy of model boats were often shown to be stitched along one side, and painted to imitate cowhide. They were probably designed to carry spears. This type of quiver was almost certainly used on Egyptian river vessels, where it would have been secured to the outer panels of the boat cabin.

During engagements, arrow quivers were placed on the ground at the feet of archers, who appeared stringing their bows. Archers were often shown with their quivers placed in pairs on the ground. The cases were placed upright, so that the archers could easily bend down and select the weapons required.

SOLDIERS AND HATCHETS

During the Middle Kingdom, both functional and model axes were placed in the graves of males, females and children. Although they were often interred as individual objects, axes were included among weapon groups. Axes also continued to be used in amuletic contexts, and miniature hatchets were worn around the neck. Various axe types are depicted on Middle Kingdom coffin panels.

Fig. 50: Silver was used in the manufacture of this large epsilon axe that is housed in the British Museum; it was probably ceremonial in nature. This type of axe can be compared with the combat weapons used by soldiers at Beni Hasan (Fig. 47). *(Bridget McDermott/ British Museum Collection)*

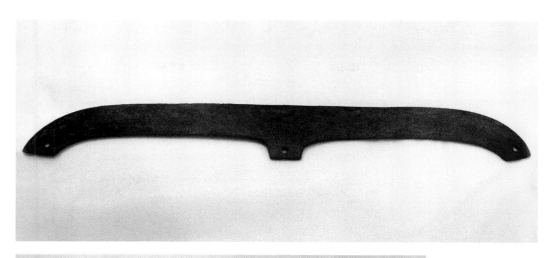

Fig. 51: Varied types of axe that were mounted on short and long staves were used for slashing and hacking. *(Bridget McDermott/ British Museum Collection)*

An examination of the vast remains of Middle Kingdom hatchet blades has produced the most comprehensive analysis of any ancient Egyptian weapon type. Middle Kingdom axes were made of bronze and copper; stone axes were manufactured throughout the Middle Kingdom and early 13th Dynasty. Precious metals such as silver were used to decorate ceremonial weapons (Fig. 50).

Several Middle Kingdom axe types have been examined and identified by the British Egyptologist Vivian Davies (Fig. 51). The first has a thin, fully rounded blade and was designed with lugs or protrusions. In most examples, the hatchet blade has been manufactured with three perforations. The second axe is similar to the first, designed with hooked lugs and with a segmented, crescent shaped blade. The third variation is designed as a slashing axe, with both symmetrical and asymetrical blades. All of these axes have shallow, wide cutting edges. A further variant is designed with a concave butt. A raised central rib often strengthened the blade. Only those that are symmetrical in form have lugs. Yet another example of the Middle Kingdom axe is designed with tangs, usually three in number, each perforated with one or more holes. This type is indistinguishable from the Asiatic epsilon axe, but the other varieties, which include the crescentic form with the long central tang, the wide-edged crescentic form and the shallow form with a straight cutting edge, are all Egyptian in origin. Axes with single lugs are rare. The wide-edged crescentic varieties always have flanges on the rear edges and the straightedged blade usually retains a central rib. Their hafts were often well protected and the blade was often attached or guarded by rivets. Lugs are consistently present only on the wide-edged crescentic form, and then only when the method of hafting was lashing. The tanged crescentic hatchet became the traditional battle-axe of the Middle Kingdom.

Through scientific analysis, Davies noted that specific types of axe were designed for military purposes. He identified a high percentage of tin-bronze and arsenic in the blades of battle-axes, while tools of this type were manufactured with blades containing a low percentage of arsenic-copper. The battle-axe was therefore relatively lightweight. Slashing axes were often classed as a hard-edged fighting baton. All three types are shown in their symmetrical and asymmetrical forms. Davies dates slashing axes to the First Intermediate Period, or early Middle Kingdom. The Asyut blade was armoured and secured by metal wiring. Rounded axe blades were mounted on long poles and used in the same manner (Fig. 52).

Anchor axes were also used during the Middle Kingdom, while eye or Asiatic fenestrated axes were brought to Egypt by foreign couriers, but were not

Fig. 52: An example of a rounded axe blade mounted on a long pole. *(Bridget McDermott/British Museum Collection)*

Fig. 53: The hafts of some axes were perforated so that a leather thong or strap could be inserted, and were curved to provide a better grip. *(Bridget McDermott/Museo Archeologico, Florence)*

adopted on a large scale by the Egyptian army. The haft of the Middle Kingdom axe was secured with linen or plant material to create an efficient grip. The haft was often curved, allowing the soldier to obtain a proficient swing and to prevent the weapon from slipping in the hand (Fig. 53). Straps were added to the axe handles of this period.

Tanged axes of the Middle Kingdom are frequently depicted in hieroglyphic texts and depictions of soldiers armed with axes are common throughout Middle Kingdom finds. From the tomb of Antef we see siege scenes that are clearly based on archaic artistic formula. Here infantrymen are shown bearing axe-blades of both the epsilon and crescent forms. Marching soldiers are depicted with their axes pressed against their shoulders or raised above their head. A fragmentary relief, dated to the reign of Mentuhotpe Nebhetepre, illustrates the

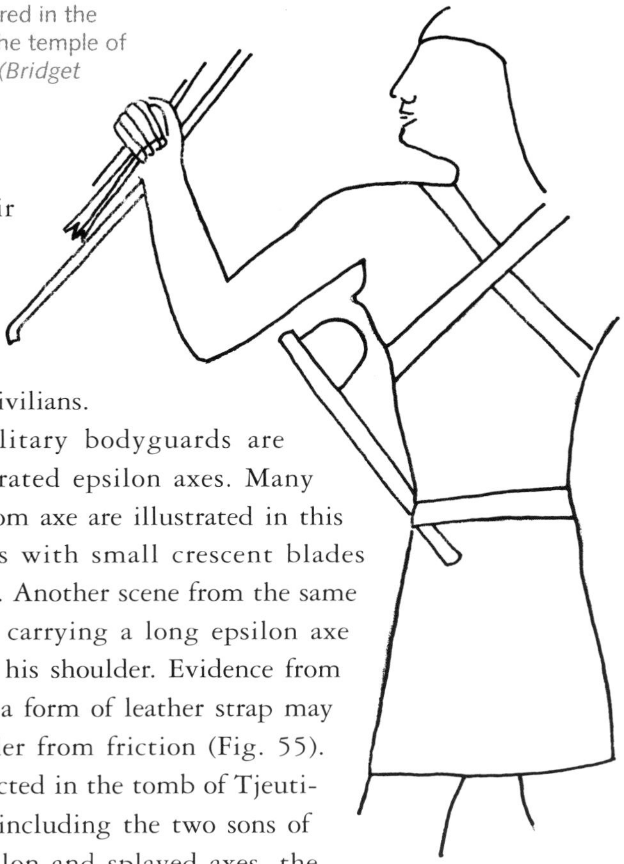

Fig. 54: The axe was often secured in the back of the soldier's kilt. From the temple of Mentuhotpe II at Deir el-Bahri. (Bridget McDermott)

way soldiers inserted their weapons in body straps and kilts (Fig. 54). The practice of securing the axe against the body was also adopted by civilians.

At el-Bersha, two military bodyguards are depicted with dual perforated epsilon axes. Many varieties of Middle Kingdom axe are illustrated in this tomb, including hatchets with small crescent blades attached to decorated hafts. Another scene from the same tomb shows a bodyguard carrying a long epsilon axe with the haft balanced on his shoulder. Evidence from these scenes suggests that a form of leather strap may have protected the shoulder from friction (Fig. 55). Three types of axe are depicted in the tomb of Tjeuti-Hetep. A military escort, including the two sons of Tjeuti-Hetep, carries epsilon and splayed axes, the latter carried flat across the shoulder with the blade turned upright (Fig. 55). The first soldier, Ab-Kau, son of Sep, carries a dual perforated epsilon axe, the binding on its shaft clearly distinguished. The second axe is designed with a small crescent blade and the haft is painted with a zigzag motif, a type of decoration found on many excavated remains.

It is most probable that the soldiers employed to protect river vessels were armed with hatchets while soldiers equipped with axes were also employed to accompany hunting parties. Model figures of soldiers recovered from the tombs at Beni Hasan were armed in a similar manner. Hatchets were included among the arms of military personnel depicted on Middle Kingdom stelae.

During the Second Intermediate Period representations of soldiers and their weapons are few. However, those remains which have been examined by Davies indicate that axes were usually lugged with splayed blades or incurved sides. This type of axe can be seen on a bovine skull dated to the Pan-Grave Culture – which is exhibited in the British Museum.

Fig. 56: The Meserheti model, found in the tomb of a prince of Asyut, shows a group of pikemen. The soldiers are armed with the traditional weapons of the infantryman, the spear and shield. Each spearhead is attached to the pike with a gut thread. Their shields are painted in black and tan to imitate cowhide. *(Bridget McDermott/Egyptian Museum, Cairo)*

SOLDIERS AND SPEARS

During the Middle Kingdom, the majority of spearheads were designed with a flat or voluted tang with round or leaf-shaped points. Such spears were probably thrown from close range. The Egyptians used volute spear tangs curved at the rear to prevent the staff from splitting as it was thrust. The widest point of the staff would be split down the centre and the tang inserted. Its volute was turned outwards, and the blade was bound with sinew or other animal remains. This type of spear can be clearly identified among the weapons of the Egyptian infantrymen depicted on a model found in the tomb of Meserheti (Fig. 56). The Meserheti Model replicates the long leaf-shaped blades, which are shown bound

Fig. 57: This model from the tomb of Meketre shows a man placing a spear at the neck of a butcher as he drains blood from the throat of a cow. During the Third Intermediate Period and onwards the spear was associated with mythical powers, a belief that may have originated during the Middle Kingdom. *(Bridget McDermott/Metropolitan Museum of Art)*

to the spear shaft by thread. In this instance, the infantry carry their spears in their free hands. These spear staffs, when held upright, are shown to measure the full height of the soldier and may have reached 1.5m or more.

From the Middle Kingdom there is also evidence to suggest that the design of the spear was subject to modifications which resulted in the production of the close combat javelin. The javelin quickly became a traditional thrusting and dual-purpose weapon. The design of the javelin differed from the spear structure in various ways. Its length often varied, allowing the infantryman to carry numerous light javelins in a quiver on his back. Further, the javelin was reinforced with a wooden or metallic grip, which acted as a counterpoise against the weight of the blade. It also enabled the soldier to jam his weapons in the ground in preparation for use. The grip also allowed the thrower to retain the end of the staff in his grasp. The javelin was often crafted with a two edged blade and a long diamond shaped tip. There is some evidence, too, to suggest that a second type of javelin was crafted, this time without a blade. Instead, these weapons were made of wooden staffs that were sharpened and tapered at the extremity. Although several examples have survived, it is difficult to ascertain their classification as staves. It is possible that these objects were javelins whose blades have not been found. The length of both spears and javelins vary enormously. For example, the short javelin may be compared with the tall spears carried by military bodyguards at el-Bersha. Here Ab-Kau, son of Sep, carries a long, body-length spear with a long leaf-shaped metal head, while the soldier who marches behind him carries a spear with a much smaller blade.

In a religious context, during the Middle Kingdom it is possible that the spear became an object of worship. Its religious connotations are revealed in scenes of bloodletting. A butcher's model from the tomb of Meket-Re shows a single male pressing a spear into the hollow of a butcher's neck as he collects the blood of a garrotted cow (Fig. 57). This scene may reflect the cultural practices of ancient bloodletting rites common among African tribes when certain metals or weapon types were used in the butchering of animals.

During this period there is evidence to suggest that iron was used in the manufacture of spearheads. The earliest known iron spearhead was produced during the Middle Kingdom and was dated by Petrie to the 12th Dynasty; it was found at the fortress of Buhen, in the shape of a broad-leaf blade. Iron was called the 'metal of heaven' because for a long time the Egyptians knew only meteoric iron, which has a high nickel content. For this reason, it is possible that iron tools were used for the 'Opening of the Mouth', an important funerary ritual performed on ancient Egyptian mummies. Sophisticated mythological interpretations of warfare and combat emerged during the Middle Kingdom military climate, and weapons such as spears were now included among the burial equipment of the upper classes. The material value of weapons is apparent, but it is evident that acts of violence and warfare were expected in the afterlife, and those dwelling in the underworld, both gods and humans, were well prepared and equipped for war.

Artistic representations of spears from the Middle Kingdom can be found in the tombs of el-Hawawish and Baqt III at Beni Hasan where they are depicted being carried by bodyguards and soldiers. Distinguishing spear types in these paintings proves problematic, as they are often difficult to differentiate from tall staves (Figs 41 and 34). However, four soldiers in the lower register of this tomb clearly wield short staves and spears. In two instances the spear is used to dispatch enemy soldiers. Here the soldier uses both hands to propel the spear into the body of his enemy and in one instance the soldier impales the enemy on his spear (Fig. 41). In comparison, the tomb of Khety yields only two tentative examples of the spear being used in battle. Here, two males are shown: one soldier carries a long spear, while another bears a sharpened javelin or stave. The representations in this tomb also highlight the introduction of the metallic or wooden handgrip that helped the soldier to retain the javelin in the hand.

During the Middle Kingdom, the spear was used by soldiers who were employed on riverboats in their role as bodyguards or ship's protectors and the mid-range capability of the spear made it an ideal weapon for such purposes. The soldier was equipped to deal with attacks from the riverbank, or on the river itself. The spear was also utilised by doorkeepers and guards. There is no evidence to suggest that these men held military posts, although it is possible that some soldiers performed these duties. Javelins were stored and transported in large hide quivers. Spears were stored in large bundles. These long cylindrical containers are depicted loaded with large numbers of long and short javelins, their heads often visible at the lid. Large cowhide spear cases were secured diagonally to the frames of boat canopies.

SOLDIERS AND MACE

During the First Intermediate Period, hieroglyphic signs show the archer resting the mace on his shoulder. During the Middle Kingdom the function of the mace remains unclear although some scholars have suggested that it was retained for ceremonial usage alone. Only a single representation, in a tomb at Beni Hasan, shows the military function of this weapon while the military role of the mace continued to be illustrated through temple, tomb and coffin decoration. Remains frequently occur

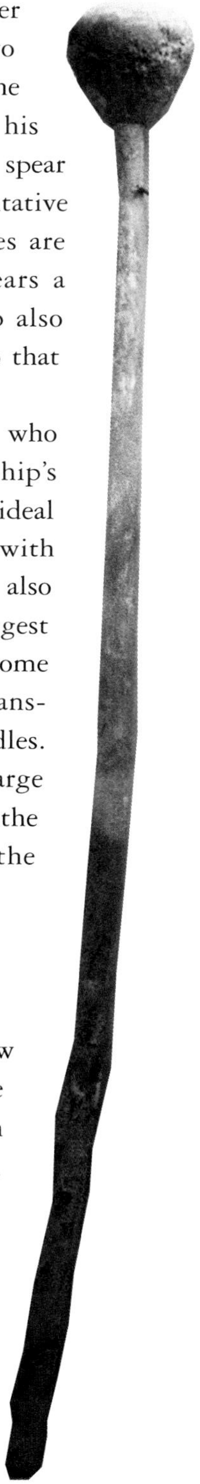

Fig. 58: A unique example of a pear-shaped mace mounted on a long stave. (Bridget McDermott/Museo Archeologico, Florence)

Fig. 59: These throwsticks were given grips of leather or thread. *(Bridget McDermott/ Egyptian Museum, Cairo)*

among funerary deposits, and that new developments were being initiated seems clear from the fact that one example of a mace-headed weapon has been recovered mounted on a long stave (Fig. 58).

SOLDIERS AND THROWSTICKS

The appearance of throwsticks among weapon collections is evident during the Middle Kingdom. These objects were depicted in a military context or commonly placed in graves and tombs. Two throwsticks were recovered from excavations dated to the 12th Dynasty. An example of a throwstick crafted with a pronounced handle was recovered from the Ramesseum, while a shorter example that was labelled as a child's toy was decorated in red chevrons and dark dots. The remains of gut thread found among or wrapped around throwsticks is not uncommon (Fig. 59).

It has proved difficult to identify the precise role of the throwstick and its function during the Middle Kingdom. Although some scholars have suggested that it was used as a hunting weapon in the same way as the Aboriginal boomerang, there has never been any evidence that this type of weapon existed within the military structure of ancient or modern Africa. If the boomerang did exist in ancient Egypt, one would expect it to have survived among modern arms, for the continuity of ancient prototypes in this sector remains common.

Although Petrie discredited accounts of the use of the throwstick before the 12th Dynasty, artistic representation during the Middle Kingdom period reveals that it was employed during armed conflict. While throwsticks were shown on the painted walls of the nomarch's tombs at Beni Hasan, a soldier depicted on a limestone fragment from Buhen is also armed in this manner. During the Middle Kingdom jointed throwsticks were employed and continued in use during the New Kingdom Period.

THREE

New Kingdom Warfare

A Brief History of the New Kingdom Warrior Kings

The Hyksos

The Egyptian New Kingdom provides scholars with an abundance of written and pictorial accounts of Egyptian warfare. During this phase the Egyptians established well trained armies that were commanded by the sovereign and patronised by the chief god, Amun. As Amun gained in power, one cannot fail to recognise some aspects of religious fundamentalism in the Egyptian campaigns. It is clear that the Egyptians came to view their military expansion as a religious crusade – and in doing so, they marched under the banner of Amun.

Amun, whose name means 'the Hidden One', was often depicted as a man wearing a double feathered crown (Fig. 60). A statue of the god was kept in a granite shrine deep in the heart of the temple at Karnak; cloistered in the darkness, he awaited the daily rituals of regeneration enacted for him by the High Priest. In return, he offered the Egyptians military victories and unprecedented wealth. He delivered both in abundance. Amun worked on behalf of the king, his mission to 'extend the borders of Egypt' – the Egyptian army executed the will of their sovereign and god by marching into territory deep in the heart of Nubia. In the north, the army focused on Asia, and would eventually travel beyond the Euphrates, and in the west, they would come to dominate the peoples of Libya. Although the Egyptians would trade, intermarry and exact taxes from the people who lived beyond their borders, trading with Canaanites, Asiatics, Hurrians and Hittites, they would always mistrust foreigners and refer to them as nonentities. In texts they were called 'the vile Asiatics' or the 'wretched foe', and the faces of bound foreigners were painted on the floors of Egyptian palaces to be trodden underfoot. Because of their distaste for foreigners, the Egyptians made the different races of people easily identifiable on the walls of their tombs and temples. The figures are provided

Fig. 60: Amun and Hatshepsut, detail from a New Kingdom obelisk.

Welcome daughter of Amun Re. You have seen your administration in the land, you will set it in order and repair all that is in ruin. You shall strike the Libyans and smite the troglodytes – you will cut off the heads of the soldiers you capture. Your tribute will be many men for the temples of the two lands and you will place offerings in Thebes at the steps of the king, Amun Re, Lord of Thebes.

From Hatshepsut's Mortuary Temple at Deir el-Bahri. *(Joann Fletcher)*

Fig. 61: Asiatics depicted during the reign of Ramesses III. *(Bridget McDermott/Egyptian Museum, Cairo)*

with distinctive features, so that each race is presented with specific characteristics. The Nubians, for example, are always shown with large earrings, short curled hairstyles and prominent noses. The Asiatics (Fig. 61) were portrayed with long cloaks and pointed beards. As if to underscore their identities, the separate races were painted on specific walls of the Egyptian temples that faced the countries from which they originated.

Although the 18th Dynasty emerged from the ashes of the Hyksos wars, Egyptologists still know little of this dark phase of Egyptian history. During the Second Intermediate Period, a group of people known as the Hyksos are thought to have settled in the Egyptian Delta having come from the Levant in search of grazing land for their cattle and for trade. Over a long period, these nomads began to settle in Egypt and acquire land. Egyptologists have indeed established that a large population of Asiatics was living in the north-east Delta long before 1674 BC, where they were mixing and intermarrying with native Egyptians. Around 1700 BC these groups established political control of the north and went on to found a fortified captial, Avaris, in the Delta region.

At one time it was thought that the Hyksos invaded Egypt. A quotation from 'Aegyptiaca', a work compiled by the Egyptian historian Manetho, who lived during the third century BC, seems to substantiate this hypothesis:

> Tutimaeus. In his reign, for what cause I know not, a blast of God smote us; and unexpectedly, from the regions of the East, invaders of obscure race marched in confidence of victory against our land. By main force they easily overpowered the rulers of the land, they then burned our cities ruthlessly, razed to the ground the temples of the gods, and treated all the natives with a cruel hostility, massacring some and leading into slavery the wives and children of others. Finally, they appointed as king one of their number whose name was Salitis. He had his seat at Memphis, levying tribute from Upper and Lower Egypt, and always leaving garrisons behind in the most advantageous positions.

Egyptologists now discredit the invasion theory and some aspects of Manetho's account, which was written long after the period of Hyksos rule. Instead, they site evidence to suggest that the Hyksos infiltrated Egypt over a period of many years. It is clear that the Hyksos ruled from the Delta and controlled Memphis; they also forged alliances in the south with the kingdom of Kush, which lay above the second cataract in Nubia. The Egyptian rulers, who retained their hold on Thebes, were trapped in an impossible situation between the two states. Petty feuds between the two rulers were common. Once, the Hyksos king Apophis ordered the Egyptian prince Sequenenre II at Thebes, to close his hippopotamus pool because the animals were keeping him awake at night – Apophis lived several hundred miles away!

Sequenenre II died violently before the age of thirty. His skull, now exhibited in the Egyptian Museum in Cairo, shows terrible injuries that had been inflicted by the blow of a hatchet and other blunt weapons. It is possible that he died during the war with the Hyksos. While the Thebans had clearly organised a resistance against the invaders, their chances of success were limited. The Hyksos knew their enemy and its territory. They were masters of the horse and chariot and employed experienced bowmen proficient with the composite bow. Unlike the Egyptians, who still wore fabric body armour, the Hyksos wore metal helmets. The Thebans, however, were enraged by their occupation, and a fierce sense of national identity proved a powerful weapon. Kamose, the son of Sequenenre II, established an army and carried out military raids. He dispatched a fleet of boats to the north carrying weapons and soldiers. In an effort to expand his territory he destroyed the Hyksos rule in Middle Egypt. It was to be his successor, Ahmose, who would conduct the final assault. Ahmose planned to fight the Hyksos in the northern Delta, where the occupiers would find it difficult to mobilise their chariotry. In an account of these battles, a soldier, Ahmose son of Abana records:

Now, after his majesty had slain the Asiatics, he proceeded to the river Khenthennefer to destroy the Nubians. His majesty made a great slaughter among them. Then I took captives there, two living men and three hands. I was presented with gold in double measure along with two female slaves. His majesty sailed down-stream, his heart full of joy and victory, for he had seized Southerners and Northerners.

The Hyksos were expelled from Egypt and driven back into Sharuhen in southern Palestine. Many of the Asiatics remained in Egypt, and the Egyptians used their knowledge of metallurgy and military technology to strengthen their own capabilities. Military imagery was embraced by the state, and appeared on large scale monuments. It produced a strong psychological effect, promoting the prowess of the king and hinting at the divine intervention of Amun. Ahmose was now in a strong position. He had liberated the Egyptian people and had established a firm leadership, providing land grants for his soldiers and presenting fabulous rewards in return for the loyalty of his officials.

Egypt's Warrior Kings

The New Kingdom produced many outstanding warrior kings. Some of these rulers were military men who had royal connections or were married to royal women. Among the former, Tuthmosis I began his career as a general. He may have been forty years of age when he came to the throne, taking the title 'Mighty Bull', an epithet that was adopted by other rulers of the 18th Dynasty. Tuthmosis campaigned beyond the third cataract in the south and conquered the Kushites who had caused so many problems for Kamose. Tuthmosis was astute; he realised the importance of his initial campaigns and enlisted trustworthy members of his family to govern Egypt while he was abroad. He established Thebes as the new capital of Egypt where he erected monumental

buildings, a practice that was emulated by later kings of the 18th Dynasty. He was also the first king to build his tomb in the Valley of the Kings.

A soldier employed in the army of Tuthmosis I pays tribute to his king, saying:

He brought the ends of the earth into his domain. He reached as far as its extremities with his mighty sword, seeking battle, but he found no one who could face him. He penetrated the lands that were unknown to his royal ancestors.

Fig. 62: Soldiers are depicted in large numbers on the walls of Hatshepsut's temple at Deir el-Bahri. Here soldiers are shown marching with palm fronds as a sign of their peacetime role during this expedition to Punt; however, the plants are balanced with weapons and military standards. *(Bridget McDermott)*

His son, Tuthmosis II, died at an early age, having made successful incursions into Palestine and Nubia. He built magnificent military ships and established effective new policies that required that the sons of conquered chieftains be educated at the Theban court. Here they would have attended the temple schools and been absorbed into Egyptian life – such men would sometimes join the Egyptian army and be promoted to high ranks within the regime. He died without an heir. Tuthmosis had a daughter by his Great Royal Wife, but it was his secondary wife, Isis, who bore the male child. He too was called Tuthmosis. The boy's stepmother and aunt, Hatshepsut, was appointed as co-regent until he came of age. Hatshepsut, who had been daughter, aunt and stepmother to two Egyptian kings, took her place on the throne. She was reluctant to give it up. In the second year of her reign she declared herself pharaoh and ruled Upper and Lower Egypt successfully for the next eighteen years.

Egyptologists have supposed that a bitter feud existed between Tuthmosis III and the new ruler as he grew into manhood. Some scholars believe that he made vicious assaults on her monuments after her death. The very fact that Tuthmosis survived his aunt may bear some reflection on her humanity, and subsequently shed some light on the relationship that existed between the two. While Tuthmosis gave all his energy to the military, little is known about the policies of Hatshepsut, although there is some evidence that she may have led at least one military campaign. Her mortuary temple at Deir el-Bahri has yielded vivid

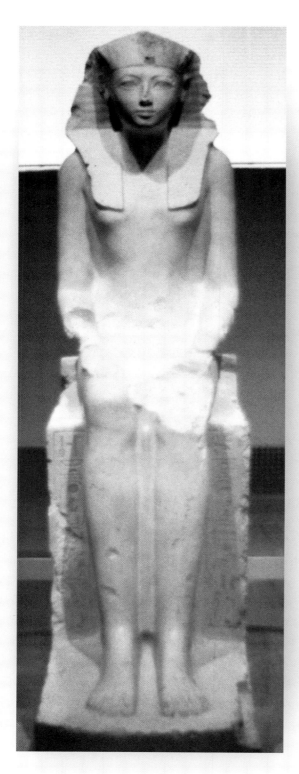

Fig. 63: Hatshepsut.

Words spoken by Amun, lord of the gods, 'Behold, my daughter Hatshepsut, may she live. May you [the gods] be pleased with her, and be satisfied with her.' Words of the gods to Amun Re: 'This is thy daughter Hatshepsut, may she live, we are satisfied, let her live. She is the daughter of your form, you have given her your soul, your margin and the power of the diadem.'

Hatshepsut's Mortuary Temple at Deir el-Bahri. *(Joann Fletcher/ Metropolitan Museum of Art)* images of the military (Fig. 62). Here, soldiers are shown on the prows of boats, and accompanying a trading expedition to the land of Punt where the Egyptians traded luxury goods. Detailed representations reveal soldiers leading exotic animals while others bear mascots, standards and weapons (Fig. 119).

Ancient Egypt has produced little evidence regarding the role of women in times of war; they are known to have accompanied the army on the march, and were employed in domestic contexts. There were, however, several female rulers who inherited the throne during times of conflict, including Queen Sobeknerefru of the Middle Kingdom whose titles describes her as a female pharaoh, and Tetisheri, the mother of Sequenenre II. A Middle Kingdom woman, known as Senebtisi, was discovered buried with full military regalia, including a kilt that had martial features. Nefertiti, who is now believed to have ruled Egypt after the death of her husband Amenhotep IV, was depicted smiting the heads of the enemy in a traditional pharaonic pose. While these images are rare, Egyptologists have discovered a small limestone fragment that reveals the image of a woman firing a bow from a chariot. The depiction is so obscure that scholars have assumed that it is simply an illustration of a story or myth.

While Hatshepsut (Fig. 63) lived, and enjoyed a peaceful reign, Tuthmosis concentrated on his military career. He was a pious man who gave a great number of donations to the temple of Amun. Perhaps, like Alexander the Great several centuries later, he really believed in the stories of his divine birth. Tuthmosis III proved himself both as king and commander of the army. When he came to the throne he was a confident man who was fully prepared for his role. He set out immediately on a series of campaigns that were recorded in fine detail in the Annals of Tuthmosis III. The king was also an explorer and an adventurer. Like Napoleon, who would one day execute similar policies in Egypt, he made detailed drawings of the plants and animals he found in foreign territories and reproduced them on the walls of the Egyptian temple at Karnak. The representations have survived and can now be seen in an area known as the Botanical Gardens.

The Annals provide historians with the first detailed account of a major military campaign. The 'chief military scribe' of the Egyptian army was responsible for keeping a detailed diary of events. These texts were kept in an archive in the Temple of Amun at Karnak, while excerpts were inscribed on its walls. By examining these reports, Egyptologists have been able to analyse the king's campaigns, producing fascinating records of the movements of the Egyptian army during their operations. Tuthmosis led a well trained army that was able to live off the land and survive on natural resources. As they marched the army drew water from the wells that had been dug along the desert roads.

En route for his famous battle at Megiddo, Tuthmosis and the Egyptian army left the fort of Tjel on the 25th day of the 4th month of winter, year 22 (of the King's reign). The Egyptians covered a distance of 201km to Gaza in 10 days, arriving on the 4th day of the 1st month of summer, year 23. These details suggest that the Egyptians marched on average 20km per day, over desert roads. They stayed in Gaza for one night, setting out for Yehem the next day. Here they camped for several days, conducting scouting operations, then on the 16th, a war council was held, and the leaders of the army decided which route to take to Megiddo.

The king's advisers expressed their doubts about the chosen route to Megiddo. The narrowness of the 'Aruna Pass, which led directly to the Qina Valley, became a matter of concern. The narrowness of the pass, only 9m wide at some points, and several kilometres long, could leave the Egyptians vulnerable to attack at the rear before the head of the army had even reached the valley beyond. Details of the king's reaction to his men's concerns are typical of New Kingdom royal rhetoric. The king is shown to stand alone, his decisions opposed by his men. He makes a confident speech that highlights the incompetence of his soldiers – the men, inspired by his bravery, reaffirm their loyalty and commitment, and rally around their leader with a new-found faith.

In reality the king's decision to choose the 'Aruna route was a brilliant move. If another path had been taken, the army may have found itself at a great strategic disadvantage, allowing its enemy time to take evasive action. The 'Aruna Path took the army directly to Megiddo, allowing Tuthmosis to lead his force into a valley behind the enemy line, outmanoeuvring them and trapping the Syrians.

His Majesty proceeded in a chariot of electrum [an alloy of gold and silver], with all his weapons of war, like Horus, the Smiter, lord of might; like Montu of Thebes, while his father, Amun, strengthened his arms. The southern branch of his army was on a hill south of the river of Qina, the northern branch was at the north-west of Megiddo while his Majesty was in their centre, with Amun as his armour, and valour in his limbs. Then his majesty prevailed against them at the head of the army, and when they saw his majesty, they fled to Megiddo in fear, abandoning their horses and their chariots of gold and silver.

As the enemy soldiers retreated, they reached the city of Megiddo which had been closed against the Egyptian army. The king watched them as they were heaved up the walls by ropes made of clothing – and no doubt with great loss of dignity.

> The people hauled them up, pulling them up by their clothing into the city; the people of this city had closed it against them.

At this point, the Egyptian soldiers lost control and began to plunder the battle site, causing a serious delay in the King's progress. Tuthmosis was forced to order a siege of the city; it would be seven months before the enemy surrendered.

> Now, if only the army of his majesty had not given their hearts to plundering, they would have captured Megiddo then. When the wretched foe of Kadesh and the wretched foe of this city were hauled up in haste to bring them into the city. The fear of his majesty was in their hearts, their arms were powerless, the serpent diadem was victorious against them.

After conducting seventeen campaigns, Tuthmosis III died in 1436 BC after a reign of fifty-four years. He was succeeded by his son Amenhotep II. Amenhotep erected a monument on the north-east side of the Sphinx at Giza, which describes his great skills as an archer and horseman. He conducted three campaigns in Asia, during the third, seventh and ninth years of his reign and the campaigns are recorded on tablets. While historians have made much of the cruel acts perpetrated by Amenhotep, his brutal reactions, which included mutilation and mass public executions, were not unique.

> When his majesty returned with joy of heart to his father Amun, he slew with his own weapon the seven princes who had been in the district of Tikhsi, and had been placed head downward at the prow of his majesty's barge. One hanged the six men of those fallen ones before the wall of Thebes.

The Egyptians had a history of violent aggression. They were not averse to impaling prisoners and inflicting facial mutilation. They were also known to burn prisoners alive. To the Egyptians, who placed so much emphasis on the preservation of the body, the latter punishment must have seemed the most abhorrent end of all. During the following event, Amenhotep II was perhaps re-enacting an old Canaanite rite called *herem*, which involved the sacrificial burning of prisoners.

> Then two trenches were made around them. Look, they were filled with fire. His majesty stood guard over them till the light with his battle axe in his hand.

During the seventh year of his reign, he campaigned to the north, crossing the Orontes, and reaching Kadesh, where he took part in the hunting expedition that would become mandatory after every victory.

As Mitanni, the Kassite dynasty at Babylon, grew in political stature, the Egyptians and the Hittites were no longer the two dominant powers in the region. Now, they were aware, one country could form an alliance with the other and act against them. This situation brought about a period of stability, when each region began to appease its neighbour. Trade flourished and the Egyptians entered into the most prosperous period of their long history. They traded with Babylon and Ugarit. Caravans brought leather and wool from Syria, while wine and timber were imported from Lebanon. The Egyptians traded, too, with Crete, Napata, Anatolia and Naharin – their merchants and messengers travelled as far as the Euphrates bearing greetings, gifts and the letters that passed periodically between the various royal families. Diplomatic marriages were arranged, and foreign brides were brought by convoys of soldiers to the land of Egypt where they would be established in the harems of the royal court. As the Egyptian king enjoyed a life of great wealth and luxury, he turned his attention to the building of monuments that were designed on an unprecedented scale. The military for a short period of time, seemed redundant. The man who ruled Egypt during this magnificent epoch was Amenhotep III known as the Sun King (see under 'Revolution', p. 122). The next military leader to emerge from this phase was the army general, Horemheb.

After a period of internal conflict and military restrictions, Horemheb and his army were once more looking towards war. Horemheb, who liked to be depicted as a scribe, was an accomplished administrator. In the temple of Karnak, he published a series of reforms on a massive stele which was over 5m high. Here, he declared his intention of instilling discipline into the troops, and he established new regulations regarding the conduct of soldiers that, if broken, would be punishable by exile or execution. He planned two centres of training for the army – one to be situated at Thebes in the south, while the other would be built at Memphis in the north. He appointed two viziers to control respectively Upper and Lower Egypt. To tighten his political grip he made the viziers military commanders, and the High Priest of Amun directly answerable to the king. Horemheb also wished to be known as a great speaker for the Egyptians greatly admired skilled orators. In the aftermath of the Amarna Period, it is not surprising to find that the king of Egypt placed great emphasis on justice and military capability – in the crisis that had ensued, it had taken a skilled and courageous leader to eradicate the memory of the reign of the heretic King Amenhotep IV, and his legacy of profound instability.

Horemheb had no heir. It is hardly surprising that he chose a military man to succeed him. His position would have been authorised not only by the king, but by oracle of Amun. That man was Ramesses I and he became the first ruler of the 19th Dynasty. Very little is known about him other than that he came from the north of Egypt. Ramesses was old when he came to the throne, and the reign was brief. His son, Seti I, was also a soldier. On his succession Seti immediately began to initiate his building programme; he chose to construct his cenotaph at Abydos, the cult centre of Osiris. He also began work on his tomb, which remains one of the finest burial sites in the Valley of the Kings at Thebes.

In the first year of his reign he embarked on a campaign into Sinai. Seti led the army as far as Tjel, a fort station at the end of the well-trodden Horus road. The Egyptians, who had previously built water wells and fort stations along the route, found that many of the buildings were occupied by foreigners. Seti was forced to secure these stations before he marched on to Gaza. From here, he lead his army to Megiddo, following in the footsteps of his ancestor Tuthmosis III. He arrived at Beth-Shan which was situated south of Lake Galilee, and from here the army took northern Palestine and campaigned far into Lebanon. In the following years Seti I advanced towards the Orontes and the army penetrated Kadesh – the gateway to Syria. There, Seti engaged in a battle with the Hittites led by their king, Mursilis. Although Seti was victorious he knew that it would be impossible to retain control over the area, so he settled for the official recognition of an Egyptian boundary in southern Kadesh.

Seti's son, Ramesses II (Fig. 64), is the most famous of Egypt's kings. A teenager when he inherited the throne, he succeeded his father in 1279 BC and reigned for a period of sixty-seven years. He built many magnificent temples in Egypt and Nubia, and his presence can still be felt on a grandiose scale. His military expeditions began early and his first Syrian campaign was undertaken during the fourth year of his reign. His army marched from Tjel to the lands of Canaan, Tyre and Byblos, and then advanced eastwards towards Amurru. After

Fig. 64: Ramesses II, Egypt's greatest military leader, from the statue at Luxor Temple. *(Bridget McDermott)*

the allies of the Hittites surrendered to Ramesses, he returned in triumph to Egypt via Phoenicia. He soon became restless again. Now, over-enthusiastic and full of confidence, Ramesses launched an offensive against northern Syria. He set out from his capital Piramesse in the Delta, and marched through Canaan, reaching the River Jordan. He continued towards Kummidi, passing the Beqqa Valley, and finally arrived at Kadesh, a strategic location situated between Lebanon and Anti-Lebanon. Here, the army, which was travelling in four separate divisions, confronted a formidable enemy force.

Now the wretched foe from Hatti had come and brought together all the foreign lands to the end of the sea. The entire land of Hatti had arrived, the Naharin too, that of Arzawa and Dardany, that of Keshkesh, Masa, Pidasa, Irun, Karkisha, Luka, Kizzuwadna, Carchemish, Ugarit, Kedy the entire land of Nuges, Mushanet and Qadesh. They covered the mountains and the valleys and were like locusts in their numbers. He [the foreign king] had left no silver in his land. He had stripped the land of all its possessions and had given them to all the foreign countries in order to bring them with him to the battle.

Ramesses had received information from captured spies that the Hittite king was encamped with this massive army a good distance from Kadesh. With growing confidence he pressed his forces on. The information was false. The Hittite army lay in ambush behind the hills of Kadesh. They let the first Egyptian army division pass, and then attacked the second.

They came from the south of Kadesh, and attacked the division of Re in the centre – they were marching unprepared. Then the infantry and the chariotry of his majesty was weakened, while his majesty was camped at the north of the town of Kadesh on the west bank of the Orontes. They came to tell it to his Majesty. His Majesty rose like his father Monthu, siezing his weapons of war. He took his coat of mail, he was like Baal in his hour. His horse, 'Victory in Thebes' was of the stable of Usermmatra-Setepenra, beloved of Amun. His majesty drove him at a gallop and charged the forces of the Hatti foe, being alone, no other with him. His Majesty proceeded to look about him and found 2,500 chariots attacking him, all the fast army of the foe and his allies

Alone on the battlefield, with his shield bearer, Menna, Ramesses pleaded with Amun for divine intervention.

I call to you my father Amun
I who am among a host of hostile forces
All countries are against me
I am alone, there being none with me
I call for them, but they ignore me
The troops have deserted me, not one of my chariotry looks for me
I shout for them
But they do not heed my call . . .
Now, though I prayed in the distant land
My voice resounded in On
I found Amun came when I called to him
He gave me his hand and I rejoiced
He called
Forward, I am with you
I, your father, my hand is with you,
I prevail over a hundred thousand men
I am lord of Victory, who loves valour

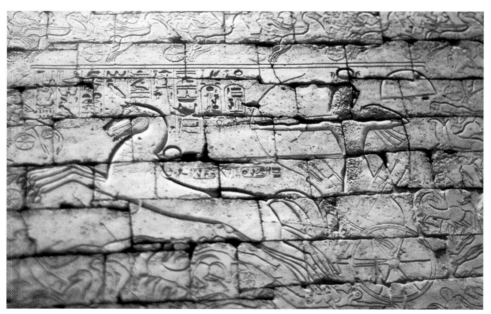

Fig. 65: Ramesses II depicted in his chariot. This image was used to emphasise the might of pharaoh as army commander. He is traditionally shown crushing the enemy under the hooves of his horse. *(Bridget McDermott)*

The Egyptian chariots were lighter and more agile than those of the Hittites, which carried three men rather than the Egyptian pair. In this way, the Egyptians had a small advantage. Ramesses drove off the enemy troops until reinforcements arrived, and pushed the Hittites back (Fig. 65). The following day, the Hittite king, Muwatallis, sent his messengers to the Egyptian king to request a truce. While Ramesses would always claim that the Egyptians were victorious at Kadesh, it was the Hittites who enjoyed the benefits of the battle's aftermath. Ramesses had survived an ordeal that obviously had an enormous impact on his psyche – for it is interesting to note that he would avoid the site of Kadesh for the rest of his life. He soon lost the Egyptian province of Upi in the region, and later the Hittites were able to reclaim their territory from the Egyptians.

Ramesses went to great lengths to display numerous images of the battle of Kadesh on many of his monuments in the Theban area and beyond. In these representations images were accompanied by an inscription that described the battle. The king, the largest figure in the scene, always took the central place in the narrative. His horse is shown with its legs raised as if it were about to trample the enemy soldiers. The battle scene unfolds before the king, showing groups of warriors engaged in combat. Egyptian soldiers are presented in small groups of three or four, their shields raised in uniform solidarity. Foreigners are depicted in large, chaotic groups being trampled to the ground.

The mortuary temple of Ramesses II was known as the House of a Million Years and contains several depictions of the battle camp. The king's tent is revealed surrounded by activity. In each section a scene associated with the battle is enacted. The Hittite spies, who presented the king with false information, are portrayed being beaten by Egyptian soldiers. Here, the enemy attack is shown alongside scenes of the feeding of animals while archers can be seen casually stringing their bows. Individual scenes are highlighted. Soldiers are shown engaged in marching drill, while the treatment of wounded men is clearly depicted alongside equipment piles and ration stores. All the scenes are dominated by the onslaught of the Hittite chariots, which are executed to emphasise the shock tactics of the enemy as they bear down on the vulnerable king.

Due to the uncommon length of the reign of Ramesses II, his son, Merneptah, came to the throne at a very late age. Written evidence shows that he was immediately faced with a Libyan invasion. It describes how he was forced to deal with an army of 25,000 enemy soldiers as they advanced upon the Delta accompanied by their families and possessions carried in carts pulled by oxen. During his reign, Merneptah would deal successfully with periodic waves of

Fig. 66: Merneptah, the son of Ramesses II. *(Bridget McDermott/Egyptian Museum, Cairo)*

Libyan invaders who were desperate to find agricultural land. The Libyans are always shown as dark skinned people who were hunters and cattle breeders. The Egyptians depicted them with their hair braided into a side-lock. They were shown naked except for a cloak and a penis sheath. The Libyans fought with bows and javelins, but their chariots were heavy and no match for the Egyptians. Bands of Libyans were divided into tribes which the Egyptians identified as Tehenu, Libu and Meshwesh.

Merneptah's (Fig. 66) reign was brief, no more than ten years, and a group of short-lived kings succeeded him. Internal conflicts were made more problematic by the constant feuds that erupted among the Theban priests. Once more, central authority was weakened. At the dawn of the 20th Dynasty the last of the great warrior pharaohs, Ramesses III, took the throne. Profoundly influenced by his ancestor Ramesses II, he sought to emulate his achievements by adopting his titulary and reproducing certain facets of his building programme. However, Egypt no longer enjoyed unlimited wealth, and Ramesses III was unable to build on the same scale as Ramesses the Great. Desperate for land, the Libyans reappeared in the Delta and Ramesses was forced to deal with their rebel armies. In an ancient ceremony Amun has presented the king with a sacred scimitar and assured him of victory. Before going forth into battle, the king would make a speech to rally the troops. The officers of the king reply to the call: 'your war cry encircles the sun. The shade, cast by your sword, is upon your army, and they go forth, imbued with your power'.

The Egyptians with their light chariots, composite bows and large armed forces conquered the Libyan people, taking numerous prisoners, including women and children who were pressed into the workforce as slaves. The enemy soldiers were taken away in shackles, their flesh branded with the name of the Egyptian king.

The Sea People were another enemy. It is thought they originated in Anatolia and that they had travelled through Syria with their families in carts. Another branch of these invaders arrived by sea via Crete. The Sea Peoples, who had already invaded the city states of Syria, seemed invincible. Later, they would settle in Palestine, which took its name from one of their group, the Peleset. The Egyptians engaged them on land and sea. On the land the Sea Peoples made war using chariots and tactics that were similar to those adopted by the Egyptians. Their sea vessels were propelled by sails rather than oarsmen, and the Egyptians confronted them at the mouth of the Delta. The Egyptians stationed lookouts on the masts of their ships, and slingmen were positioned in crow's-nests, hailing stones down upon the heads of the invaders. The Sea People rammed and forced their boats into the rivulets of the Delta where the Egyptian bowmen attacked them from the shore. Ramesses said that a net had been prepared for the enemy, and that they had fallen into it – and there they were butchered without mercy.

The pictorial representations of the battle have survived in the Temple of Medinet Habu (Fig. 68) which contains more than 7,000m^2 of inscribed stone. It has an original fortress gate which stood on the main quay where the temple could be accessed from the river. At the front of the temple there is an elaborate guard house, its walls decorated with scenes that illustrate the king crushing the traditional enemies of Egypt. The outer walls of the temple were covered with battle scenes showing the campaigns of Ramesses III against the Libyans and the

Sea Peoples. The first court has scenes showing the Egyptians counting the severed hands of prisoners, while on the south wall, stick-fighters and wrestlers are presented in combat displays. Above them, a window known as the 'Window of Appearances' can still be seen from which the king would have bestowed prizes and gifts on his officers. The representations at Medinet Habu (Fig. 67) depict the last great military scenes of ancient Egypt. Here, a unique scene shows elite members of the army issuing equipment to the troops. Above it, the king's words are recorded: 'Bring forth weapons! Send forth the army to destory the rebellious lands.' The walls of Medinet Habu (Fig. 68) remain one of the most important and fitting monuments to the Egyptian army, and to the ancient art of war.

THE MILITARY LIFE

The elite members of the ancient Egyptian army were highly educated. Although such men were trained to fight on the battlefield, they also worked as military scribes and officials who dealt with the logistics of warfare, namely transport, rations and the general mobilisation of large contingents of men. They used their skills in reading, writing and mathematics to establish a finely tuned militia. From as young as five years old, boys of upper-class families were expected to attend school where they would learn from anthologies or 'school books' compiled by teachers. The remains of these books reveal a little of the attitude of the schools towards the military. During the New Kingdom, the military had become an important institution, and ranked alongside the administrative and religious sectors in professional standing. For this reason, the school books, known today as The Miscellanies, focused on the negative side of military life in order to persuade young boys to join the scribal profession. In this text, the life of the soldier is described.

> He is brought while he is a child in order to imprison him in a barrack. An agonizing blow is given to his body, a heavy blow is given to his head. His head is split open with a wound. He is laid down and is beaten like a strip of papyrus. He is crushed with the beating. Come – let me tell you of his going to Kharu, and about his march upon the hills; his bread and his water are upon his shoulder like the load of a donkey. His neck is rigid, like that of an

Opposite, above and below: Fig. 67: The army of Ramesses III marches out to fight the Sea Peoples. They are armed with shields and khepesh swords. *(Bridget McDermott)*

Fig. 68: Medinet Habu, Temple of Ramesses III. In the background are the tombs of the nobles and the Valley of the Kings. *(Bridget McDermott)*

ass. His back is broken. He drinks polluted water and stops only to stand guard. He reaches the enemy while he is like a pinioned bird. If he succeeds in returning to Egypt he is like a stick that has been eaten by the worms. He has fallen sick. He is seized in a paralysis, and he is brought back on a donkey. His garments have been stolen and his retainer has abandoned him.

Although The Miscellanies provide us with important information regarding the type of difficulties the soldier might face, the military life also had many benefits. Although a soldier's life was arduous, we must assume that descriptions such as that above were exaggerated; the Egyptians described many professions including those of butcher, merchant and farmer in this way in order to emphasise the comparative benefits of becoming a scribe.

Fig. 69: Stick fighters were employed during festivals and victory celebrations, and probably performed duels as a part of the funeral rites of royal persons. This scene is from Medinet Habu. The Egyptians staged duels and displays of armed combat during state ceremonies and events, which is a tradition that is still adhered to in modern Egypt. *(Bridget McDermott)*

Conscription and Training

There were two ways in which infantrymen were obtained for military service. Although some positions in the army were hereditary and one could volunteer for an army career, many men were conscripted (Fig. 70). It is clear from a New Kingdom text that even candidates for the priesthood could be conscripted as soldiers.

The vizier brought three youths, saying, 'Put them to be priests in the Temple of Hetephermaat-Merenptah, in the house of Ptah!' but they were siezed and taken away to the north, one was saying 'they shall be infantrymen!' Indeed, may you hurry and go after them, and write their conditions.

Fig. 70: Men are shown being conscripted into the army in the tomb of Userhet at Thebes. Here, soldiers are shown seated and are about to have their hair cut or inspected for lice. *(Bridget McDermott)*

After the Amarna Period, it is possible that the Egyptians developed a specific division that employed priest soldiers. Some priests were depicted and buried with weapons while a specific unit of bowmen, shown on the walls of Medinet Habu, are dressed in priestly attire.

Men remained in the army throughout their lifetimes: veterans often came to be known as 'aged' infantrymen; they made a living from farming. However, military representations always show soldiers at the height of their physical prowess; only rarely, as on those representations found on the wooden chest of Tutankhamun, are signs of age visible on the faces of Egyptian soldiers.

The recruits were assigned to two major centres, one in the north, the other in the south of Egypt, for military training. The Miscellanies describe the training of the soldier in the following way:

> He is thrashed to exhaustion. He awakens in the morning only to receive beatings until he is split open with wounds. He is equipped with weapons upon his arm, he is standing on the drill field every day. A painful blow is given to his body, a powerful blow upon his head, his eyes and his nose.

There are no specific texts that deal with army instruction. However, pictorial representations depict soldiers in close drill formations, being led by unit commanders in the form of standard-bearers. These representations show well-drilled men, who were skilled in repetitive manoeuvres. Artistic representations show that sappers, who are able to scale large buildings, were well versed in the

crafting of battering rams. While it is clear that soldiers were led by trumpeters and drummers who controlled manoeuvres through signal drills, standard-bearers may have used decorated flags to lead their units on the field.

Trained soldiers can be seen on public display in representations of funerary rites or public celebrations and Egyptologists have suggested that artistic representations of these scenes reveal ancient sports or 'games'. In modern times two branches of the British army have used the construction and firing of a cannon as a traditional combat display at an annual royal event; in the same way,

Fig. 71: In the tomb of Kheruef at Thebes soldiers are shown taking part in boxing matches.
(Bridget McDermott)

it seems likely that the Egyptians may have produced images that show public displays of military manoeuvres. In ancient Egyptian art, the sports of stick-fighting, boxing and wrestling were frequently depicted among the funerary scenes on the walls of mortuary temples (Figs 69, 71, 72 and 73). These events, which may have been incorporated into royal funerals, were known in some cultures as funeral games.

Scenes of combat illustrate the traditional striking and parrying movements that are still used by modern Egyptians in stick-fighting displays, where once staves were used for beating the body of the opponent. During the New Kingdom the Egyptians designed arm boards, helmets and jaw guards to protect themselves from the blows of these weapons; however, this type of protection does not appear in military scenes. The body was protected by linen padding that was wrapped around the chest. During these games, soldiers used stalks from the palm plant as staves. In scenes from Medinet Habu, where a stick-fighting display is shown, we catch a glimpse of the reaction of the audience whose comments are recorded in the hieroglyphic inscriptions which accompany the text. Encouraging words are shouted at favoured fighters, upon whom wagers were placed. In similar scenes from the tomb of Amenmose the soldiers taunt each other: 'Be watchful, you wretched, boastful soldier', while his opponent replies, 'It is you who is a fool to lay a hand on one of his majesty's soldiers!'

Boxing and wrestling matches are depicted both at Medinet Habu and in the tomb of Kheruef at Thebes. The inscriptions that occur among these scenes show the words associated with the modern sports, such as to strike and to defend. Another sport with a direct military application was target archery, which was important in the training of young archers. The introduction of the composite bow meant that a new generation had to learn both traditional and advanced techniques. Scenes show trainers standing behind young candidates, correcting posture and issuing instructions; for example, in one

Fig. 72: In this scene dated to the 20th Dynasty two soldiers are shown engaged in a duelling match. They wear tall conical helmets and adopt armguards to protect them from the blows of their opponents. *(Bridget McDermott/Egyptian Museum, Cairo)*

Fig. 73: This scene which is dated to the Amarna Period shows the use of linen binding to protect the body during combat. (*Bridget McDermott/Louvre Collection*)

scene a trainer corrects the archery stance of a young boy saying, 'Pull the line to your ear. Keep strong your arms. Act with force and strength' (Fig. 74). Having accomplished a basic training in archery, the boys of upper-class families would then progress to practise archery from a moving vehicle, from which they would shoot at standing targets. New Kingdom kings were skilled in all forms of combat. The archery technique of one pharaoh was described in the following way:

> Entering his northern garden, he saw four targets of Asiatic copper assembled for him. One was a palm in thickness and placed at a distance of twenty cubits between one target and the next. His majesty appeared on his chariot like Montu at the height of his power. He pulled the bow while holding four arrows in his hand. He rode northward, firing at them, like Montu in his battle-dress, each arrow piercing the back of the target as he fired at the next. This deed had never been done – shooting an arrow at a target of copper, so that it came out and fell to the earth.

The Soldier in Peacetime

When not required for military engagements, the standing army was used in various ways. Egyptian written texts often show soldiers being used to transport building materials, or to protect mining expeditions which often took large groups of men to Egypt's borders with foreign lands. These expeditions, which required manpower on a massive scale, were accompanied by military scribes, sometimes twenty in number, who would distribute rations. Soldiers were employed to retrieve escaped prisoners, and are often shown with dogs who were specifically trained for scouting missions. Groups of armed men were also sent to foreign countries as part of a retinue; for example, they would accompany the processions of concubines who were regularly sent to the king of Egypt as the gifts of foreign rulers.

The Soldier in Battle

Before the army set out on campaign the Egyptians conducted an official ceremony in which military units were acknowledged by the gods. The term 'anointing of soldiers', used in official texts, is a reference to the ceremonial recognition of the troops as they left for war. Here, the public appearance of the king was also acknowledged. 'Pharaoh, has appeared at the beginning of the Day of Appearing, on the day of commanding to Heliopolis to perform the purification ritual.' A list of oils that were said to have been used to anoint the king's army have been found in these ancient texts.

The army paraded in their divisions, including infantry and chariotry. Recent examinations of New Kingdom reliefs also reveal mounted soldiers who were armed and carried quivers. Egyptologists have failed to discern the presence of a cavalry among the ranks of the Egyptian army; although mounted horsemen are attested (Fig. 75), they are generally classed as scouts.

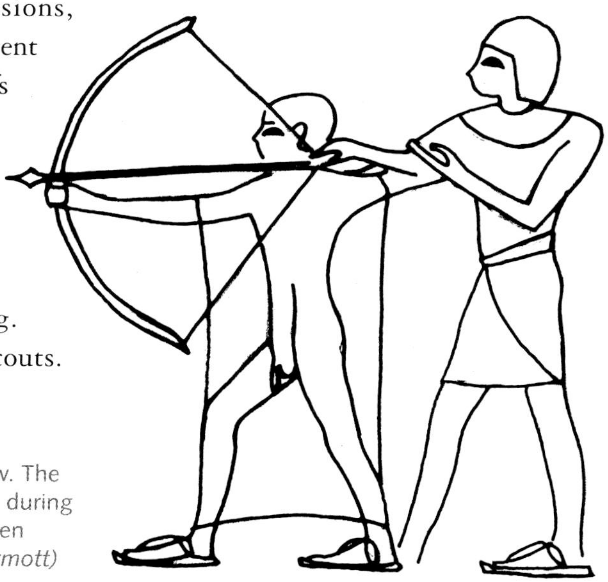

Fig. 74: Amenhotep II learns to use the bow. The Egyptians used wooden and copper targets during archery practice. They also used targets when practising from the chariot. *(Bridget McDermott)*

There were two types of soldier: one section of the infantry comprised professional soldiers, while another group, like the modern territorial army, were viewed as recruits who were only called up for service during periods of conflict.

The chariotry were an elite division of the army who provided tactical support to the troops. It seems to have been distinguished from the traditional units of the military, and acted as a special division. The infantry, who were trained in hand-to-hand combat, were also employed as sappers, and were fully trained in

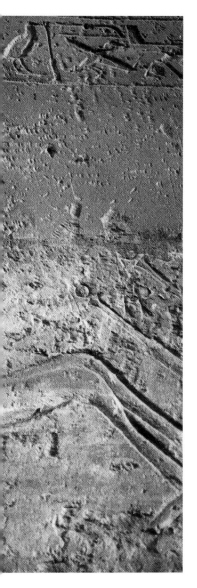

Fig. 26: During the reign of Ramesses II and Ramesses III there were numerous depictions of the Egyptian army engaged in siege warfare. Here, in drawings taken from reliefs of the Ramesside Period, the soldiers of the army of Ramesses III are shown providing protective cover for sappers. Soldiers fell trees in order to make siege ladders, while a trumpeter poised on the fort parapet directs the troops. *(Bridget McDermott)*

Left: Fig. 75: Although scholars dismiss the use of cavalry units within the ranks of the Egyptian army, horsemen are commonly depicted. During and after the Amarna Period, men armed with bows or staves are shown on the battlefield mounted on horses. This mounted soldier of Ramesses II is on a wall in the Luxor Temple. *(Bridget McDermott)*

siege operations (Figs 76 and 89). Light infantry are always shown armed with spears, shields and auxiliary weapons. Armed men are depicted on horses in several representations that date from the Amarna Period onwards and it is likely that these men served important roles on the battlefield. Companies of archers and mercenaries were divided into separate units led by standard-bearers who carried the emblems of the field. The Egyptians relied on river transport for the moving of large groups of soldiers, animals, chariots and weapons, although there is no evidence to suggest that the Egyptian army trained marines. While military terms highlight the role of soldiers who were connected to specific ships, and who engaged in combat on water, there is no evidence to suggest that they received a specific training for this type of fighting.

During campaigns, which included extensive marches, the Egyptians would have made a basic camp that meant sleeping in the open. They kept warm by maintaining braziers and sleeping under blankets (Fig. 77). Tents were erected for the elite members of the army, whose accommodation was attended to by servants and bodyguards. The army was accompanied by cooks, doctors and scribes. The campaigns would also have attracted traders, metal workers and female servants. In all probability, women would have worked as prostitutes. Children are likely to

Fig. 77: This fragment (below), dated to the Amarna Period, shows soldiers sleeping under blankets. Soldiers keep warm by a fire (left). *(Bridget McDermott/Brooklyn Museum)*

have been employed as servants, and artistic representations show them in this role. An established battle camp, that is a camp that remained a permanent feature during a military engagement, would have proved more elaborate. It was probably entrenched, having been built within a perimeter fence that was guarded by armed sentries placed at each quarter of the enclosure. Within the camp, a war industry thrived. Horses and equipment were attended by specialists, and units of soldiers would have had space to prepare themselves and drill. The king and his attendants would have lived within leather tents, and one area would have served as a counsel apartment, where the king or his general would eat and discuss their options, receive foreigners or conduct war counsels. The camp may have included a public podium so that the king could address his troops. Indeed this type of address is attested to; on the eve of a New Kingdom battle of Tuthmosis III, the king's speech included the words 'equip yourselves and sharpen your weapons'.

Military Standards

The practice of bearing military insignia is as old as war itself. Although standards were a sign of regimental affiliation, they were also used to send signals and identify manoeuvres used by units on the battlefield. Ancient Egyptian standards in the form of flags or totems, were decorated with various images that included wrestlers, ships, plumes, horses and lions. A unit that carried the symbol of a horse was not always connected to a chariot corps – it is more likely that standards may have been connected to a locality. Four separate standards, used for the major army divisions, were associated with the gods of Egypt, each section fighting under the banner of Ptah, Amun, Seth or Re.

Medicine and War

Although The Miscellanies exaggerate the difficulties of life in the military, the logistical problems faced by large groups of Egyptian men marching over long distances must have been great. The texts indicate that dysentery, lice and water pollution were all problematic issues. Artistic representations from the tomb of Userhet also reveal groups of soldiers being inspected for lice. The soldiers would also have suffered from severe foot problems, and it is no surprise that in military texts his staff and sandals are listed among the most important items belonging to the soldier. In scenes from the battle of Kadesh, guards are shown sitting on quarter stones being attended by doctors who examine their feet. While written evidence regarding the treatment of battle wounds is limited, the Edwin Smith Medical Papyrus provides reference to symptoms and treatments connected to wounds sustained in combat. Gaping wounds were associated with the head and the area around the eyes and seem to have been treated by the application of fresh meat, oil and honey. Wounds to the nose, ears, lips, throat and shoulders are also discussed. The Egyptians would most likely have stitched gaping wounds and bandaged others with linen strips. Infected wounds would have been treated with herbs that were probably administered through a base oil called Moringa. Plants such as thyme and cinnamon were used as antiseptics, while aloe was applied to burns and inflammation. Mandrake root was taken as a narcotic. Fractures were also common; they were treated with manipulation, splints and swabs.

Rewards

The service of an Egyptian soldier was rewarded with land endowments and the land would remain in the possession of the family – just as long as the men were available for service. The soldier's performance on the battlefield seems to have been measured by the human remains he recovered. After slaying an enemy soldier he would sever various parts of the body, usually the hand; and would attach these remains to a rope-coil that he wore upon his body. In his tomb biography, Ahmose son of Abana, having brought back a series of hands, was rewarded with slaves and land.

Prisoners of War

The counting of prisoners was a frequent feature among the artistic and literary representations of war. The Taking of Joppa was an Egyptian story that reveals a strong similarity to tales from the Arabian Nights. Here infantrymen hid themselves in baskets and were carried into an enemy city. The soldiers were armed with fetters and slave collars, which they would use to bind captured prisoners. Similar fetters, which were also made of wood, can frequently be seen around the necks and wrists of prisoners depicted on the walls of Egyptian temples. Artistic images also show the branding of Egyptian prisoners, possibly with the cartouche of the king or a temple emblem. Papyrus Harris records that the human herd, or foreigners, were 'branded and made into slaves, they being stamped by my name, their women and children being dealt with likewise. I brought their herds to the House of Amun, they being made for him as cattle forever.'

The Military Hierarchy

The king as the unchallenged commander of the army would be assigned to a chariot corps during his youth and would accompany his forces on major campaigns. He had his own chariot and horse team, sometimes distinguished by name. Although we have little evidence of the role of the king in battle, it is unlikely that he was placed in immediate danger. Although he often proved himself a fine athlete, seemingly imbued with superhuman prowess, he would have been protected by a wall of bodyguards and his welfare would have been paramount. As he grew older, it is probable that he would have passed his role as commander on to his son and heir.

The king would set up battle camp with his soldiers and conduct conferences with his counsel in his war-tent. He would have been accompanied by his general and army commanders. Under the generals, infantry commanders or officers were employed to control the units of infantrymen. Officers of this type could take command of specific forts, and in this role they were known as the fortress-commandant. Next in the military hierarchy was the standard-bearer, who would lead a company of soldiers. Beneath him was the common soldier, or the *w'w (aha)*, who bore several titles during the New Kingdom.

The army was identified by its divisions, each named after an Egyptian god. During the battle of Kadesh, the divisions were named after Amun, Re, Ptah and Seth. Each division comprised a complete army unit and bore an epithet or a motto. Epithets include such aphorisms as 'a multitude of heroes' or 'strong of bows'. Studies have suggested that each division was made up of 5,000 common soldiers, 20 officers and 20 scribes. Individual companies of men were made up of 250 people, each company being divided into 5 platoons of 50 men. Each company or squad had a specific title, for example, 'The Aton is Resplendent' or 'Beloved of Amun'. The titles seem to have had great significance, and they were traditionally preserved over long periods of time.

According to Alan Schulman, a leading authority on Egyptian military titles, the army was contained within four areas: the Army of Kush in Nubia; the army of Syria; and the Home Forces, which were divided into two sections, Upper and Lower Egypt. One unit was positioned in the Delta. During the late New Kingdom, a series of forts was constructed on a military road that crossed from the Delta into Asia, enabling the Egyptians to take control of Lower Egypt. These garrisons would have provided the army with water and rations and also functioned as lookout-posts where men would record the activities of foreigners and control trade. Recruits may have lived in the communities that sprang up around the garrisons and were called up at times of unrest.

In representations of military engagements the infantry are always depicted in hand-to-hand combat and there are also instances where they are shown as phalanx soldiers, providing a strong, uniform image of Egypt's finest warriors. They are further depicted as sappers, conducting operations against the fortified strongholds of enemy states. This type of soldier was probably placed at the front of the offensive formation. As a group, the movements of the infantry were controlled by trumpeters, who are often shown on the parapets of siege towers, sending signals to the army below. The standard-bearer, an elite member of the army, would direct and contain the unit with the practised movements of the regimental flag. The chariotry protected the rear and flanks of the infantry. The Egyptians engaged in siege warfare when a direct assault was impossible. This procedure was often a long and complicated process, and the Egyptian army would have spent many weeks in the battle camp. During the New Kingdom it is clear that the Egyptians employed archers to protect the infantry when they attempted to lay siege to enemy fortifications; here they would assault the enemy with showers of arrows, which would be fired up at the parapets of the city wall or fort.

Logistics

Military scribes, who had a specific hierarchy with their own commanders and officers, played an important role in the administration of the army, with responsibility for providing and itemising rations for the infantry and chariot corps, keeping records of the provisions and listing the prizes of war. Scribes were also used to keep records of recruits, trace deserters and document crimes. Some scribes kept records of the events of the battle and, during the battle of Megiddo, Tuthmosis III employed his scribes to record the fauna and flora of the Asiatic regions. These records were reproduced in images in the so-called Botanical Gardens in the Temple of Karnak. Hieroglyphic inscriptions in the tomb of Tjaunny, a military scribe, describe his office: 'he recorded the soldiers in the presence of his majesty, recorded those eligible for the elite troops, and instructed all men in their military duties'.

Amenhotep, son of Hapu, renowned for his work as architect for Amenhotep III, also held the title 'scribe of the elite troops'. His work is described as 'raising up the men for the elite troops, making correct arrangements for the protection of the frontiers and superintending the prisoners of war'. Military scribes were also assigned to prisons; one title is translated 'scribe of the prison of the army', which may refer to a prison for military personnel or a holding place for foreign captives. Although army commanders fulfilled an administrative function by corresponding with other commanders, it was the job of the scribe to write the dispatches. The letter would be given to messengers who were responsible for the smooth transfer of documents from one garrison to another.

Although army scribes were controlled by a commander it is unlikely they saw combat. Scribes were employed in the Broad Hall of the Palace, a title that probably refers to the official military headquarters that were established at different sites in Egypt. Here a law court was set up for military hearings, and it was here that soldiers were 'equipped with all their weapons'. This type of hall is depicted in a unique scene from Medinet Habu which shows a weapons store and the issuing of arms (Fig. 78).

The soldiers' rations included linen, bread, corn and ointment. The men paid for these rations with wooden tallies that were designed in the shape of bread loaves. In Papyrus Lansing it is said of the soldier that

He receives the corn-ration when he is released from this duty, but it is rank when it is ground. There are no clothes and no sandals, the weapons of warfare are at the fortress of Tjel. During his march, he drinks water every three days, it tastes like salt. His body is crushed. The enemy is here, and surrounds him with arrows, his life is far away. They say, 'Quick, valiant soldier, win for yourself a good name!' But he does not know himself. His body is weakened, and his legs are feeble.

Fig. 78: The temple of Medinet Habu was designed with a large ceremonial hall from which weapons of war were issued to the army. In this unique scene the soldiers are shown with angular bows and quivers. Khepesh swords are shown with looped handles. Cap helmets are being carried by soldiers; one of the helmets is depicted with a band that indicates that it was worn by a unit leader. (Bridget McDermott)

Another version of this text continues 'the foreign woman has fainted through marching and he puts her around his neck. His kit is dropped, as he is loaded with the captive. His wife and children are in their village; he is dead before he reaches it.'

Soldiers were expected to stand trial for their crimes which included the stealing of hides and food. Although looting was an acceptable practice, it was expected that prized objects should be returned to the state. At the battle of Meggido soldiers were berated for their looting, a practice that resulted in the escape of the enemy and forced the Egyptians into a long and complex siege operation. Serious crimes included desertion. In one text it is stated that 'he is fled and gone away amongst the deserters, whilst all his family are confined in jail. Now he is dead upon the desert, and there is no one to carry on his name'. When scribes arrived at an estate to enlist soldiers, a number of people were known to have run away in an attempt to avoid the draft. Even commanders were subject to the law and were punished for the abuse of soldiers under their command. Many references that describe the life of the soldier highlight the harsh beatings and discipline that was required during military training. Scouts with tracking dogs were employed to track deserters, whose families were imprisoned for their crimes. A text that deals with this problem states:

> I came to the place in which my lord was. It is so that the infantryman of the area was seized, the one whose field work was assigned to me. Someone has given him to the prison in the village and he is cultivating the land on behalf of the army scribe Pamerka who lived in the village of 'tbnt'.

Concepts of Valour

There is little emphasis placed on the ideology of valour among Egyptian soldiers. Unlike the Greeks, the Egyptians did not highlight acts of individual courage in official inscriptions, instead they drew attention to the actions of the king, the commander in chief. However, personal bravery is highlighted in several military texts. For example, in several biographical accounts, men describe themselves as 'valiant before soldiers' or as 'the leader of every valiant man of the army'.

REVOLUTION

Akhenaten, the second son of Amenhotep III (Fig. 79), succeeded his father some time between 1378 and 1352 BC. During the reign of Amenhotep III,

Fig. 79: Amenhotep IV wearing the traditional Egyptian war crown. *(Bridget McDermott/ Ashmolean Museum, Oxford)*

Egypt had reached the height of its prosperity and its military and political supremacy over neighbouring countries were secured. However, during this period of national stability, the country was afflicted by internal power struggles, namely a conflict between the monarchy and the priests of Amun. The power of the priests of Amun, the intermediaries between the monarch and the god Amun, now the most influential deity in Egypt, was well founded. Over a long period of national stability the priests of Amun had also amassed considerable material wealth through the taxation of vassal states.

In the second year of his reign the king tried to curb the influences of the Amun priesthood by elevating another deity, the Aten, to pre-eminence in the Egyptian pantheon. In this way he attempted to create a theological equilibrium. Later, he would go so far as to replace the god Amun, who had long been established as the supreme god of Thebes, with the Aten – the sun disc. The move had major political implications. Breaking alliance with the capital city, Thebes, Akhenaten took the unprecedented decision to establish the Aten as a supreme diety – and for the first time in Egyptian history, the general populace was faced with the concept of monotheism. In reality, among ordinary civilians, who worshipped a large and varied array of deities, this new religion had no chance of success. The events of this period are still clouded in uncertainty, but it is clear that the Egyptians attempted to wipe out all pictorial or written allusions to this dark phase of their history. After his demise, the name of the ruler was hacked from all large-scale reliefs and he would forever be known as 'the heretic' king.

In the fifth year of his reign the king had moved the court to a new city that he had had built in the desert in Middle Egypt. The site is known as Akhetaten, 'Horizon of the Sun Disc'. The city was built in an oval shaped plain, flanked by desert mountains. It stretched across 13km of the arid landscape measuring 5km wide at midpoint. The city limits were marked with fourteen boundary stelae, inscribed with an oath which the king made, never to leave the city. The population of the city was estimated at twenty thousand people who inhabited villas or small houses in its northern or southern sections. The royal family lived in palaces in the central area of the city while their tombs were cut into the surrounding cliffs.

Amun had been regarded as the 'Hidden One' and had been worshipped in dark sanctuaries in the most secret recesses of the Egyptian temples. On the other hand, the Aten, the one god, was worshipped as the visible sun disc, and his rituals were conducted in the open air, where the rays of the sun could penetrate the altars of the god. In elevating the Aten, the king had emphasised the creative force of the sun, reclaiming totalitarian power and depriving the priests of Amun of their most important role as intermediary between the ruler and the gods.

At some point early during the reign of Akhenaten there occurred an event which produced a severe backlash against the cult of Amun. Precisely what happened is still unclear, but it was most probably an assassination attempt on the king. The result was a furious attack on the monuments of Amun, where the Egyptians hammered out all hieroglyphic and pictorial references to the Theban god. In order to execute such a campaign, the king must have had the support of the military; one can only imagine the scenes at the holy city as the Theban officials faced the repercussions of their actions, and the king's wrath erupted on the people inhabiting Karnak temple.

This attempt to eradicate the old gods was unsuccessful – indeed, there is evidence that the people of Akhetaten continued to worship various gods on a personal basis, and prayers to Amun have been discovered in the workmen's village at Amarna. Such evidence may show that the people of Akhetaten worshipped in secret, or that the king's vendetta was waged mostly against the Theban priests and their cult rather than against the god Amun himself. In any event, it is clear that Akhenaten closed down the temples at Thebes, causing major disruptions to the central administration which had previously controlled the economic and political affairs of Egypt.

Akhenaten commissioned works of art that are highly distinctive. Features that have often been described as having a 'sensual realism' were unknown until this period; here the human form was depicted in a less rigid manner, the figurative lines became soft and sensual, and more emphasis was placed on the sensitive interaction between the subjects and the natural elements around them. Images of the royal family dominated the artistic creations of the period, revealing a unique sense of intimacy between the subjects. The extraordinary accentuation of these figures and the distended appearance of the human body have been the focus of academic analysis for decades.

For a long time, Akhenaten was regarded as a pacifist. Indeed, many modern esoteric societies such as the Rosicrucians consider Akhenaten a seer or a 'poet-king'. However, for Egyptologists this view is no longer viable – ironically, modern archaeological examinations have revealed evidence to the contrary. Excavations at the city of Akhetaten have produced an abundance of military reliefs and remains that prove that the army played a dominant role in activities at Amarna. In representations, the military body appears at all times during public events where it provided protection for the royal family. Military

Fig. 80: Two soldiers at Amarna engaged in conversation. The soldiers are armed with a stave that is unique to this phase. The baton, which was slightly splayed, was probably made of dried palm fibre. *(Bridget McDermott/Brooklyn Museum)*

representations at Akhetaten surpass all other ancient Egyptian reliefs in number and in places of importance in temples and tombs – it is not too far-fetched to suggest that the Amarna military reliefs share the same sinister characteristics that have been adopted by modern dictators.

Within the central city of Akhetaten archaeologists have found the remains of an army barracks. The building, which consisted of several sections, was built at the eastern edge of the city, and provided the authorities with a panoramic view of the desert plain. The military quarters were made up of three main blocks that included an area to the south which was probably used as a war room. The building, which exhibits a strong Minoan influence, housed magazines that were used for storage, extensive kitchen facilities and a porter's lodge. The excavators also discovered a large exercise area where the Egyptians would have trained their horse and chariot teams. A parade ground, with the remains of mangers and tethering stones, was found on the northern aspect of the main wall, along with stables which were constructed with a sloping brick floor. The importance of horses and chariots cannot be overestimated during this period. Indeed, at this time the horse begins to appear in grand-scale representations that include depictions of both horse and rider. Military titles, such as that of the 'master of the horse' and 'scribe of the recruits' are recorded for the first time.

Finds from the excavations conducted at the military barracks have included a number of weapons and scaled armour fragments (Figs 81 and 82). These finds also include leather tags that were once found on the uniform of an Egyptian soldier and

Above: Fig. 81: An axe, with the remains of its leather binding. *Armour/ Metropolitan Museum of Art)*

Right: Fig. 82: Scales of armour became so large that scholars believed they once decorated statues. *(Bridget McDermott/ Ashmolean Museum, Oxford.*

bear a strong similarity to the strips of leather found on an armoured tunic in the tomb of Tutankhamun. Several pieces of these leather remains, now housed in the Manchester Museum, are carefully ribbed and dyed to imitate metal scales.

After his death, Akhenaten was succeeded by a shadowy figure known as Smenkhare. Little is known of this king, but new evidence suggests that Nefertiti, the wife of Akhenaten, was probably one and the same. Scholars are still uncovering new evidence regarding the role of Nefertiti at Amarna, but artistic representations show her in the traditional pose, a smiting ruler smashing the skulls of the enemies of Egypt, and these suggest that hers was no passive role at Akhetaten. The reign lasted two years and then Smenkhare, too, disappeared. Soon Akhetaten was abandoned, and the Egyptians systematically destroyed the remains of the city. They obliterated all written references to the king, including those on their royal ancestor lists. In doing so, they hoped to destroy the king's second life and erase the name of Akhenaten from history.

Representations at Amarna

Groups of tombs dated to the Amarna Period were excavated at Akhetaten and Thebes. While the Theban tombs retain their traditional themes, the Amarna tombs are decorated with the typical features of the period. The tombs at Amarna have produced more military representations than those yielded by any other site in Egypt. Among these scenes the infantry are clearly distinguished from the elite members of the army (Fig. 83). They are always shown in small units, bent at the waist in typical postures of subordination or as pyles of running men (Fig. 106). Soldiers are depicted carrying the traditional weapons of the infantry, namely the shield and spear – although they were sometimes also armed with auxiliary weapons. The upper

Fig. 83: This drawing of Hesi, an Egyptian soldier of the Amarna Period, taken from a New Kingdom Stele from the Pelizaeus Museum, Hildesheim, shows a special kilt that was designed with a reinforced heart-shaped panel. (Bridget McDermott)

classes, who are always depicted in close proximity to the royal family, were portrayed as standard-bearers, bodyguards and commanders.

The tombs provide Egyptologists with a great deal of information about the Egyptian military during this period. They often show armouries being guarded by soldiers, or illustrate the manufacturing techniques used during the construction of weapons and chariots. In a series of unique scenes, the activity of a shield or leather working factory is clearly depicted.

THE HORSE AND CHARIOT

> Fine chariots of wood more resplendent than lapis lazuli, being wrought in gold, their 'htr' piece of gold and their having the hue of red cloth and being carved with blossoms; their floors were wrought in wood and ivory, their reins in one set, their spokes of 'pher', and poles of 'Ipu'. They were washed, stripped, leather-fitted, finished off, oiled and polished with alloys of gold.
>
> *Papyrus Anastasi IV*

The chariot first appears in ancient Egyptian literature on the stele of King Kamose. Here, the text refers to the chariots of the Hyksos, a group of peoples who invaded and ruled Egypt during the Second Intermediate Period. It is generally believed that the Hyksos introduced the chariot to the Egyptians during their occupation. However, it is possible that the Egyptians were familiar with this type of vehicle before the New Kingdom Period, when chariots may have been introduced from the Levant along with the horse. In countries such as Mesopotamia, harness animals were included in burials; although the Egyptians included chariots among tomb equipment – indeed, some tombs were designed with a 'chariot hall' – in Egypt, horse burials were rare. The horse and chariot played an important role in royal iconography. Amenhotep II, on his great stele, is praised as the trainer of his own chariot horses. Underscoring the value placed on both horse and chariot is the fact that foreigners sent gifts of chariots, and during the Amarna Period foreigners sent letters where greetings to the royal chariot teams were emphasised.

The Function of the Chariot

Written evidence suggests that organised chariot units were mobilised during the reign of Thutmosis I, when chariot divisions acted as an elite branch of the Egyptian army. Although the chariots were adopted during land battles and were effective on level terrain, they were not used during siege operations or on rocky ground. The primary function of the Egyptian chariot was to serve as a mobile firing platform, enabling the Egyptian soldier to fight at specific points on the battlefield. The chariot allowed the soldier to provide firepower in the form of discharging archery equipment from a position elevated above the enemy. It also provided a means of transporting equipment to specific areas on the battlefield and enabled the Egyptians to recover injured men from the field, or pursue the enemy as he fled from the battle. The chariot would have been used to break up enemy formations at the beginning of a battle and to form a direct wall of manpower, being placed along enemy lines. A list of equipment taken on a Syrian expedition highlights in great detail the preparations made for horses and chariots. Stable masters and grooms attended the soldiers, taking large amounts of finely chopped straw on the march. The chariots were filled with all manner of weapons, including arrows, quivers, spears, swords and javelins.

Chariot Crews

Altogether three titles for chariot crews are known: the chariot warrior, the shield-bearer and the charioteer. The title of shield-bearer may have been used by officials of the king. Menna, the shield-bearer of Ramesses II, is mentioned as the sole companion of the king as he faces the enemy alone on the battlefield.

> Menna, my shield-bearer, knew that a legion of chariots surrounded me. He became weak – his heart was faint. Terror was in his limbs. He said, 'My good lord, strong ruler, who saves Egypt on the day of battle, abandoned by his soldiers and chariotry'. His majesty said to his shield-bearer: 'Stand firm, steady your heart, I will charge them as a falcon – I will slaughter and destroy them bringing them to the ground'. His majesty rushed forward, he charged into the melee. For the sixth time he attacked them. I was like Baal on the day of power, I slew them without hesitation.

The Egyptians also employed soldiers known as runners; these men sprinted behind or alongside the chariot and were expected to wound the horses of the enemy charioteers during direct engagement. Runners are often depicted as royal bodyguards in artistic representations.

Although foreign princes requested aid in the form of Egyptian charioteers in divisions of ten vehicles, it is estimated that a chariot unit consisted of fifty cars each of which carried two crew members. While one drove the chariot, the other acted as a shield-bearing warrior armed with archery equipment. The chariot warrior was able to carry a variety of weapons including swords and axes that were kept within the chariot structure. Military reliefs often depict the soldier climbing down from the chariot and fighting on the ground; representations from the battle of Kadesh frequently show Egyptian soldiers halting enemy chariots and dragging their crew to the ground. In battle scenes the king is usually distinguished among the ranks, appearing on a chariot that separates him from his soldiers. During the Amarna Period, the royal family are frequently depicted on chariots. In The Miscellanies, the chariot is described as carrying weapons and battle equipment. The vehicle also figures in stories and myths, being used by farmers and royalty as a general form of transport.

Chariot Design

The chariot was designed with an oval shaped body frame that was crafted to be as light as possible, its most important requirements being for speed and its manoeuvrability (Fig. 84). However, the chariot soldier needed a stable platform from which to use archery equipment. The chariot was crafted from wood; it was often designed with leather features and decorated with precious metals. Ceremonial chariots were found in the tomb of Tutankhamun, where Egyptian craftsmen had decorated the vehicles with inlays of gold leaf and precious stones. Chariots of gold and silver are often mentioned in Egyptian texts, and at the battle of Meggido, Tuthmosis III commanded a chariot made of electrum.

The Egyptians built their chariots with light wheels and placed the axle of the vehicle towards the rear. The wide wheel track enabled the chariot to make sharp turns. The car was fully open at the rear and was wide enough to accommodate two persons driving side by side. The floor with its shallow, oval-shaped frame consisted of interwoven leather straps. The framework of the body had a vertical support, with two to five supports projecting diagonally from the rail of the vehicle to the axle pole, a design which provided firm reinforcement between the floor of the chariot and the pole. The wheels, their rims made of wood and leather, were placed at the back of the body. A pole was built along the under panel of the chariot supporting the floor and the axle. The horses were yoked to a pole (Fig. 85) with leather saddles and pegs; these lay along the spine and shoulders of the horses so that the driver could control their movements. The horses of the Egyptian chariot team would have been controlled by a bridle or noseband while two reins were attached to the ends of the mouthpiece. The reins were carried back to the loops on the horses' shoulders near the ends of the yoke saddles. The Egyptians used blinkers on the horses of their chariot teams.

Chariot workshops were established at major temples, and are depicted in the tombs of the nobles at Thebes; here craftsmen are shown bending and splitting the wood that was used in the construction of military vehicles. Various types of wood were used by the Egyptians in the construction of their chariots including elm, tamarisk and birch-bark, materials that have been identified during examinations conducted on the chariots of Tutankhamun. The six full-sized vehicles that were found in the tomb of Tutankhamun are important examples of Bronze Age chariots. Special units were employed to maintain the chariot; they came under the administration of the king's stable and the royal stablemaster.

It is possible that the Egyptians established two major training schools for charioteers at Memphis in the north and Thebes in the south. An equestrian division was also housed at the city of Akhetaten at Amarna. However, as units were mobilised in Nubia and in other areas of Egypt, there must have been facilities for the housing of horses and chariots at most garrisons. The stable staff, or 'servants' worked as grooms, while others were employed to build, repair and maintain chariots and their equipment. The stables employed their own scribes who were responsible for the acquisition of fine horses and chariot pieces. In Papyrus Anastasi III the cost and weight of individual chariot pieces are listed.

DIVINE WARFARE

In ancient Egyptian myth the sun god Ra was believed to have passed through the day and night in a boat. Artistic images that reveal the events of this journey play an important part in the funerary cult of the dead kings, and were placed in significant positions on walls of royal tombs of the New Kingdom. They were known as 'The Writings of the Hidden Chamber that is in the Underworld'. The journey of the barge through the underworld included the nocturnal voyage of the sun god through twelve hours or 'segments' of the night. The boat entered each phase through a gate that was guarded by a demon. Here, the elaborate and dangerous landscape of the underworld is mapped in vivid detail by the Egyptians, and each phase is clearly distinguished as the sun god drifts through its portals on a boat manned by a full crew of warriors and gods. Each hour or section of the journey through the Amduat (the

Opposite: Figs 84 and 85: These photographs highlight the light and agile features long associated with ancient Egyptian chariots. *(Bridget McDermott/Egyptian Museum, Cairo, and Museo Archeologico, Florence)*

Egyptian underworld) takes the crew through a chamber where the god and his passengers must prevail over life-threatening events – for example, the first hour is known as 'smashing the heads of the enemies of Ra'. In the middle of the journey the sun god takes the role of a candidate who is expected to pass through a ritual where his living *ba*, or spirit, is reunited with his dead body – the definitive moment of regeneration culminates in his victory over the snake demon Apep. It is only at this moment that the sun god may appear on the horizon and a new day begins.

These phantasmagorical and violent images produce a legion of creatures who bear reptilian or hybrid features. Some of the figures bear swords or daggers between their shoulders – images familiar from modern paintings by artists such as Pieter Brueghel and Hieronymous Bosch. These nightmare images were probably accurate reflections of how the ordinary Egyptian viewed his environment. To the Egyptians, images of purity and orderliness were essential to the cosmic balance, and ideally they would place these representations on public and private monuments because they believed that by painting them, the image would become active. However, in reality, the Egyptians lived in a violent world, surrounded by forces they called 'chaos'; here disease, pestilence and danger were an everyday reality. It is not surprising, then, that the rituals for creating order out of chaos should be re-enacted in the underworld, where the enemies of the gods must always be conquered. The rising of the sun, and therefore the continuation of the life-force, was dependent on this nocturnal cycle during which the gods waged war on the demons and chaotic forces of the night. The apprehension and binding of the forces of chaos is evident in the pictorial images that show the restraint of the demons of the underworld; here kneeling prisoners are depicted with their hands bound behind their backs, an iconographic image that is repeated in grandiose representations of New Kingdom prisoner processions conducted by a real life army of flesh and blood.

The battle between the gods Horus and Seth is one of the most important myths of ancient Egypt. Horus the son, and Seth the brother, of Osiris, both came to claim the office of their kinsman. There was a dispute among the gods regarding which man should take the place of Osiris and they decided to hold a competition. What followed was a series of events in which the two challenged each other in combat, their contest resulting in aggressive contact, mutilation, magical intervention and sexual humiliation. Each of these elements, incidentally, can be identified as a method used by tribal societies when initiating young men into warriorhood. Horus, who went on to win the contest, was absorbed into an important mythological relationship with the role of kingship, while Seth was to remain in the realms of chaos. He became a god of storms and ruled the desert land. He was associated with demonic symbols and was connected to the crocodile and hippopotamus, both of which share a subterranean and benign role in Egyptian mythology.

From the prehistoric period onwards the Egyptians were highly influenced by the environment around them, and this is reflected in the way Egyptian gods retain dual aspects that mirror both the aggressive and nurturing characteristics of nature. While the Egyptians worshipped Hathor as a goddess of fecundity and childbirth, she was also seen as the devourer of blood and the murderess of mankind (Fig. 86). The capacity to kill or cure was attributed to many gods of ancient Egypt. Isis, known as 'Mistress of Magic', was renowned for her ability to heal the sick. When her husband was killed and dismembered by Seth, Isis collected the torn limbs of her spouse, and regenerated his body through her magic. However, during the battle of Horus and Seth she lured Seth into a trap by changing herself into a young girl, and subsequently severed vital parts of his body.

Amun, the primary god of the Egyptian pantheon, was often depicted anthropomorphically – while he was depicted as both a goose and a ram, he is often shown enthroned as a human king. During the New Kingdom, Amun was associated with divine kingship. Each ruler included his name in their titulary; by the New Kingdom the term 'beloved of Amun' had become a predominant epithet. At this time the god Amun was thought to provide the ruler with victory in battle, and in artistic scenes he is often shown presenting a scimitar, a symbol of his might, to the king. It was believed that Amun commanded the king to conduct his campaigns, and provided divine protection for the pharaoh on the battlefield; the prizes of war were then ritually presented to the Temple of Amun at Karnak, in reality, of course, providing a vast amount of wealth and power for the priests of Amun.

In an account of the battle of Kadesh, the first recorded battle in history, the reader is presented with a formidable relationship between the ruler and the god; it is here that victory was assured through the 'strong arm' of Amun. Heading out to do battle alone, Ramesses II laments the desertion of his troops. Facing the oncoming enemy alone and unaided, he cries out:

> I know Amun helps me more than a million warriors
> more than a hundred thousand charioteers
> More than ten thousand brothers and sons
> We are yoked as one heart.

Fig. 86: On this column at the temple of Dendera Hathor is shown as human headed with bovine features. *(Bridget McDermott)*

Many gods shared warlike characteristics. For example Montu, the falcon-headed war god of Thebes, became the divine aspect of the king's vigour. Many warring cultures produce goddesses who are associated with military themes. In ancient Egyptian myth, the goddess Satis was believed to guard the southern frontiers of Egypt and is depicted by the sign of an animal skin pierced by an arrow. Anat, a warrior goddess of Syria, was adopted by the Egyptians. She was called the 'Mistress of the Sky' and was believed to protect the king during combat. Indeed, Ramesses III describes Anat as 'his shield'. Goddesses often adopt weapons of war as their emblems; for example, Neith, the Goddess of Sais, is often shown in the form of a shield with crossed arrows; in pictorial representations she is shown with a bow. However, it is Sekhmet, the lion goddess of Memphis, who presents the most ferocious image of war. The name Sekhmet means 'powerful'. As the daughter of the sun god Re, she is often represented in Egyptian literature as a heroic figure; during battle she breathes fire against the king's enemies, turning their bodies into chaff. In combat, the king associated himself with the 'rage' of Sekhmet. In an ancient story Sekhmet is sent by the gods to destroy mankind and as one of the earliest vampires in history, she develops an uncontrollable lust for drinking human blood. Furthermore, the Egyptians often referred to Sekhmet as the 'Mistress of Fine and Red Linen', a term which may be associated with the blood-drenched clothes of her enemies.

The earliest religious texts of Egypt, the Pyramid Texts, were full of violent images of destruction, cannibalism and mutilation. During the New Kingdom, we find these images in the Book of the Dead, where the gods are often armed with weapons of war and travel in boats manned by soldiers. The Egyptians regarded the realms of the dead as a reflection of the world of the living; here the deceased were susceptible to attacks by demons (Fig. 87) and could suffer a fate called the

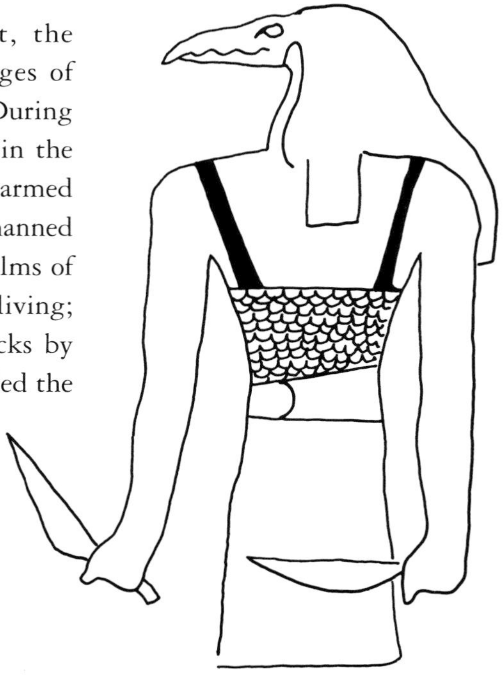

Fig. 87: The features of many demons that dwell in the underworld cannot be identified. Here a demon-headed god, armed with two knives, wears a military bodice of scaled armour, and a typical New Kingdom wig or headdress. Detail from the Tomb of Amenherkhepshef, Valley of the Queens, after Wilkinson, 2003. *(Bridget McDermott)*

'second death'. In religious literature and representation the gods are shown armed in battle with spears and knives, and are presented in various contexts, cutting off the heads of snakes or butchering pigs and reptiles. The gods, who were sometimes shown in battle scenes, adopted military clothing and carried weapons; the god Amun is often portrayed in full battle dress wearing a helmet and a corset of scaled armour. He is shown with a dagger strapped to his upper arm, and a sword tucked into his kilt. Gods are often armed with javelins. As they voyage through the underworld they strike Apophis, the chief enemy of the sun god Re, from the prow of their boat. Horus is often depicted armed with a mace and is shown engaged in the ritual slaughter of Egypt's enemies. The god of storms, Seth, appears in his role as archery tutor to Tuthmosis III. The lion god Apedamak is represented as an archer with bound captives at his feet, while the goddess Waset, an icon of the holy city of Thebes, is shown with a bow, arrows, stave and pole-axe. Demons who guard the doors of the underworld are often armed with daggers. These violent and unpredictable images highlight the awe and fear felt by the ancient Egyptians as they viewed with apprehension the natural world around them.

SOLDIERS AND THEIR ARMOUR

Head Protection

There is no evidence to suggest that the Egyptian soldier employed metallic or fabric head protection until the New Kingdom. During this period bronze helmets became an important element of the uniform of the upper ranks of the Egyptian army and at least as early as 1479–1425 BC it becomes evident that archers, among the elite Egyptian military ranks, wore helmets. It is clear, too, that the helmet became available to Egyptian soldiers during the second half of the New Kingdom (1294 BC), but during the early period it was much prized as an object of tribute and was probably worn by officers and royal persons alone. Bronze helmets first appear in the tomb of Amenmose in western Thebes where they were decorated with ostrich feathers. Among representations in later tombs (Fig. 88) helmets are depicted without ornamentation, and became more conical in appearance. During this period, helmets were kept in elaborate helmet boxes.

It has been suggested that helmets were worn by soldiers engaged in siege operations. Members of the army of Ramesses II are depicted in the Temple of Amun at Karnak wearing helmets that protected their heads from missiles being catapulted from the parapets of the fort to which they lay siege (Fig. 76). Helmets are also frequently depicted in scenes from the Temple of Medinet Habu, where

Fig. 88: Detail of a
wall painting from
the Tomb of
Rekhmire, Thebes.
(Bridget McDermott)

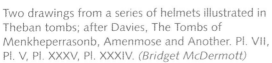

Two drawings from a series of helmets illustrated in
Theban tombs; after Davies, The Tombs of
Menkheperrasonb, Amenmose and Another. Pl. VII,
Pl. V, Pl. XXXV, Pl. XXXIV. *(Bridget McDermott)*

Fig. 89: A New
Kingdom siege scene
dated to the reign of
Meneptah, in Karnak
Temple. *(Bridget
McDermott)*

they are worn by archers and soldiers engaged in hand-to-hand combat. Head protection of this type was also adopted by stick-fighters, who are shown in traditional displays of combat (Fig. 72). A short bronze cap helmet (Fig. 90) that protected the head and the nape of the neck first appears among such representations; it was often worn with a cloth base. This type of helmet is shown on a rare fragment from 19th-Dynasty Saqqara, where a unique miscellaneous shard reveals images of soldiers weighing several metal helmets on a hand scale (Fig. 91).

Throughout Egyptian history there is little evidence to suggest that protection was worn around the facial area during combat. However, it is important to note that during the reign of Ramesses III (1186–1154 BC), a device had been developed to protect the cheeks and jaw from injury during duelling matches. There is also evidence to suggest that malachite, the thick green eye paint worn by both men and women, was used by Egyptian soldiers, most certainly by archers who would use the pigment to protect the eyes from the reflection of the sun. A kitbag, which was owned by an archer of the Middle Kingdom, yielded fragments of malachite and grease together with a small pot,

Fig. 90: This fragment, found at Saqqara, shows a series of cap helmets. *(Bridget McDermott/Egyptian Museum, Cairo)*

This unique image was found on a broken fragment at Saqqara. It shows an official weighing a group of helmets. *(Bridget McDermott/Egyptian Museum, Cairo)*

which may have been used for the preparation of eye paint. It is probable that on the march the ordinary member of the archer corps carried his equipment in this type of bag.

During the battle of Tunip, Ramesses II emphasises his decision to forego his mail coat as a sign of bravery and faith. During the New Kingdom military collars, perhaps an adaptation of the old breastplate, came into use as ceremonial garments. As an emblem of war its use was confined to royal personages. The ancient practice of binding the body with linen as a protective covering, still common among several warrior tribes in Africa, served to deflect the blows of offensive weapons and remained popular among the land soldiers of the New Kingdom. Footsoldiers carried and applied linen to their bodies in various styles, adopting no one single garment, a practice that appears again in the time of Ramesses II, where stick-fighters protected themselves with thick strips of linen which they attached to a high band worn around the upper abdomen. Corsets, presumably made of leather, are represented rarely, and may have been worn exclusively by royal and official persons. The military corset retained shoulder straps and was pulled around the abdomen and tied by cords threaded along the central panel of the garment. During the New Kingdom attenuated and sophisticated clothing such as leather corsets provided more substantial protective measures against the battering and stabbing of sword cuts and spear thrusts. Although the manufacture of metallic armour is known from the reign of Tuthmosis III, coats of scaled armour are illustrated purely as a royal garment. However, mail coats were used throughout the Amarna Period and they continued to be represented in funerary art.

Lower Body Protection

Throughout military history, the soldier's uniform often distinguishes the head or genitals in displays of male aggression. In ancient Egyptian representations, the soldier often emphasises the sexual organs by adding a distinctive sash to his kilt. It is not until the Amarna Period that a reinforced panel is established on the front of the kilt both to highlight and protect the genital area.

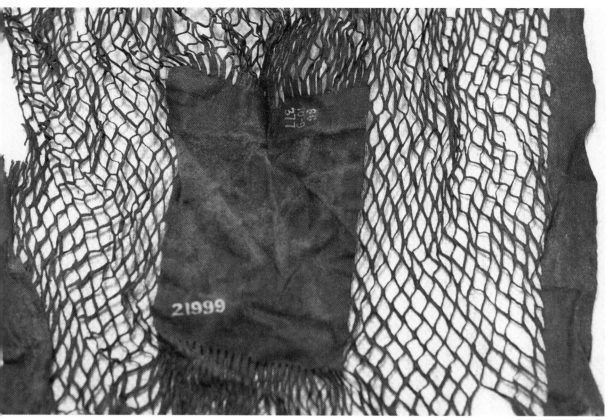

Fig. 92: The webbed cloth was worn by different types of soldiers to protect their kilts from wear. It was fastened around the waist by a thin strip of leather that was incised with holes. The kilts are often found with tail extensions. Kilts of this style were also worn during the Predynastic Period. (See those worn by the warriors of Tutankhamun (Fig. 117).) *(Bridget McDermott/British Museum Collection)*

A distinctive feature of the military uniform included the adaptation of a protective panel of leather webbing that was worn around the kilt (Fig. 92). In the tomb of Tjauny, the kilt is presented with a tail piece. This type of tail, which may have had an amuletic purpose, appeared originally on the garments of predynastic warriors and can be seen on various webbed cloths and even quivers (Fig. 108). Examination of the remains of loincloths in museum collections indicates that they are all made of a single panel of leather. A fine example of this type of loincloth made from a single length of gazelle hide was found in the tomb of the New Kingdom warrior Mahepere. It was webbed methodically, leaving a single patch of leather in the centre. Numerous fine repairs applied to different areas of the cloth are clearly evident.

Body Armour

During the New Kingdom, the shield became intimately connected with social and religious iconography. It was also imbued with amuletic properties, in which role it was designed as jewellery and was placed upon the chest of the deceased. The shield was certainly integrated into the panoply of military deities. It is evident that in this period there was an increase in popularity of war deities such as Reshep, who was generally depicted brandishing a shield and spear; increasing veneration was also associated with the Assyrian war goddess Anath, whose role as a human shield is well attested in the literary texts of ancient Egypt.

Also during this period the shield always took the form of an oval panel (Fig. 93). There were three shields represented within the artistic canon, which were depicted as embossed, rimmed with nails, or both. These shields were generally painted black or tan, either in imitation of bovine hide or in diagonal bands; in rare cases they were left undecorated. The style of the shield seems to have

Fig. 93: These shields are unique. They are made of painted wood and decorated to imitate cow hide. *(Bridget McDermott/Egyptian Museum, Cairo)*

Fig. 94: This fragment from Karnak Temple shows shields being held aloft. Wooden soldiers on the prows of model boats (see Fig. 40) are often shown holding their shields in this way. It creates a sense of action that is often lacking in Egyptian military representations. *(Bridget McDermott)*

remained relatively constant throughout the whole of this period, albeit remains are rare. During the New Kingdom, the Egyptians were still reluctant to display grandiose arms of defence within the structure of military art, and they were rarely depicted as such. Equally the Egyptian artist only rarely portrayed the necessity for defensive measures, and the shield is never executed in its true functional role. It was, however, frequently shown being held aloft in aggressive displays; during the later New Kingdom it was often represented held at arm's length, the inner area of the shield exposed to the viewer in powerful images of artistic and military confidence (Fig. 94). While the shield was the traditional arm of the land soldier or infantryman, rare illustrations of the late New Kingdom show that it was also used by standard-bearers, archers and sappers (Figs 76 and 89).

The shield of the common land soldier was manufactured with three separate panels of wood that were nailed together and covered in hide, or simply painted

Fig. 95: Shields were often embossed with metal discs. This is a detail from the court of Amenhotep III at Luxor Temple. *(Bridget McDermott)*

panels of wood in black
and tan designs. The
shield still has painted
bands around the outer rim
(Fig. 117). During the later
New Kingdom Period shields were often
strengthened with embossed discs (Fig. 95). New King-
dom shields were designed with apex coils for the attachment of shoulder
straps, and it became fashionable in siege and single combat scenes to show the
soldier with his shield slung across his back (Fig. 96). The artistic portrayal of
the soldier and his shield is often random and static, the true defensive function
of the shield rarely shown except within the context of siege manoeuvres. The
traditional New Kingdom siege scene represented on a fragment from Karnak
temple shows a soldier climbing a siege ladder laid against a fortified building
(Fig. 96). The soldier is depicted with a spear in one hand, and his shield slung
over his shoulder in a prototypical manner which can be seen repeated
throughout subsequent periods of military history. This image was to become
so popular that soldiers were satirised in the form of cats and mice who are
shown climbing siege ladders with their shields slung over their backs.

It is clear that shields were issued to soldiers by the state, their manufacture
and storage becoming the responsibility of military officials; during the New
Kingdom armouries were established at temples and forts in Egypt and abroad.
Weapons and arms were shown kept in storage in the Theban tombs of
Rekhmire and Kenamun, while a collection of elaborate shields was discovered
in the tomb of Tutankhamun (Fig. 97).

Shields belonging to the soldiers of Ramesses II that are shown on the south
wall entrance hall of the Beit el Wali temple are typical examples from this
period. It is probable that the shield was made of plain wood, which was
then gessoed and painted in various designs. The wooden shield continues

Fig. 97: These magnificent royal shields from the tomb of Tutankhamun are crafted from three panels of wood. They are overlaid with cheetah skin. *(Bridget McDermott/Egyptian Museum, Cairo)*

to imitate bovine hide, being decorated in black, brown and white. A new style of short shield painted with black and tan diagonal stripes also appears during this period. The use of black and tan pigments is common among ancient and modern African tribes. These colours are often associated with cattle cultures; for example, they are commonly used in the decorative themes of the Masai tribes, whose warrior culture often bears a remarkable resemblance to that of ancient Egypt. From the reign of Ramesses II onwards, the shield became an emblem of power and the deflector of chaos within artistic symbolism. For instance, during the battles of Kadesh, impracticable images of the shield were used to show the formation of walls around the king's encampment.

SOLDIERS AND ARCHERY

Bows

The marshalling place of your chariotry. The mustering place of your army, the mooring place of your ships' troops. They bring gifts to you saying, praise be. You have come with your corps of archers of savage countenances and burning fingers who march when they behold the ruler standing and fighting. Even mountains cannot stand before him. They are afraid of your awfulness.

Papyrus Anastasi III – Praise of Meneptah and of his Delta Residence

During the New Kingdom the design of the Egyptian bow went through various changes. The collection of archery remains from the tomb of Tutankhamun highlights the diversity of design that the Egyptians used in the manufacture of their archery equipment (Fig. 98). While the self-bow was retained during this period, the Egyptians had adopted the Hyksos composite bow. The angular bow was also adopted by the Egyptian army at this time (Figs 100 and 101). Its angles were formed by the stretch of the string against the stave limbs; on average the angles measured 30°. The composite bow is generally measured at 1.5m long. The bow limbs were designed with a grooved core, and were layered with a thick coating of glue and enclosed in wood and wood shavings. Bows of the double limb composite type were used in conjunction with the self- or longbow; both types have been found together in funerary deposits. Bows were commonly constructed with string notches. Although the simple bow was still retained by the military, it was frequently incorporated in ceremonial representations.

Instruction in archery began in childhood. Egyptian tomb scenes reveal that royal persons were tutored with the same techniques employed among military cadets. Curved bows are seen in the scenes of archery instruction, while a painting from the tomb of Menna depicts the use of both the double concave and straight bow during training. Archery was considered an art among the military classes, and bowmen played an important role in the early New Kingdom system – evidence that the elite status of the archer had survived. Stelae were commissioned by bowmen and became a standard item among burial equipment. Throughout all periods of the New Kingdom archers were expected to attend burials where they played an important part in the funerary ritual.

Although bows were manufactured in Egypt, they were frequently received as foreign taxes, tribute and booty. Six hundred and three bows were collected from the Libyan war of Ramesses III. Long and composite bows were often

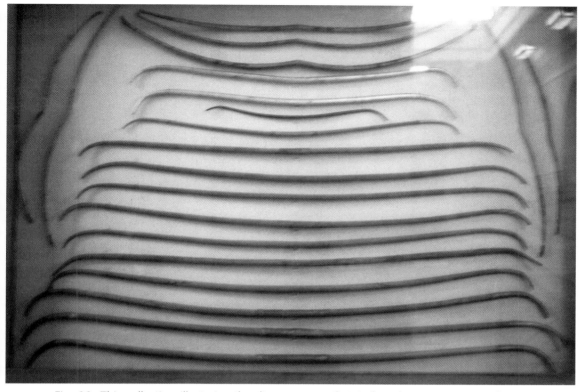

Fig. 98: This collection illustrates the diverse range that is found among Egyptian bows. *(Bridget McDermott/Egyptian Museum, Cairo)*

Fig. 99: Detail of the bowmen of Tutankhamun on a wooden casket found in his tomb. *(Bridget McDermott/Egyptian Museum, Cairo)*

found together in tombs of officials such as the fan-bearer Ahmose Penhat, while lemonwood self-bows, unstrung and 1.8m long, were found below the tomb of Senmut at Deir el-Bahri.

The iconographic presence of large phyles of soldiers was required in the innermost sanctuaries of the New Kingdom temples (Fig. 103). In the Hathor chapel at Deir el-Bahri, bowmen are shown with archery cases and quivers. They were also prolific within the configurations of the funerary art of the period; for example, bows were included among the craft-making scenes in the tombs of important men like the vizier Rekhmire. It is also possible that the bow was used in religious ceremonies during the early New Kingdom. Broken bows were found beside offering tables and among deposits discovered under the tomb of Senmut. Bows that appear in hiero-glyphic inscriptions are often shown bound. In this way the Egyptians, who believed that images could be magically activated, rendered dangerous weapons inactive.

Bowmen are often shown in funerary contexts in ancient Egyptian tombs. A bowman leading a processional phyle is shown with the double concave bow in two scenes from the tomb of Mentuherkhepeshef, where he holds his weapon in a military salute. In the

Fig. 100: The angular bow was used during the New Kingdom. It is particularly prevalent in scenes from Medinet Habu, the temple of Ramesses III. *(Bridget McDermott)*

Fig. 101: Details from Medinet Habu and the tomb of Menkheperrasonb. *(Bridget McDermott)*

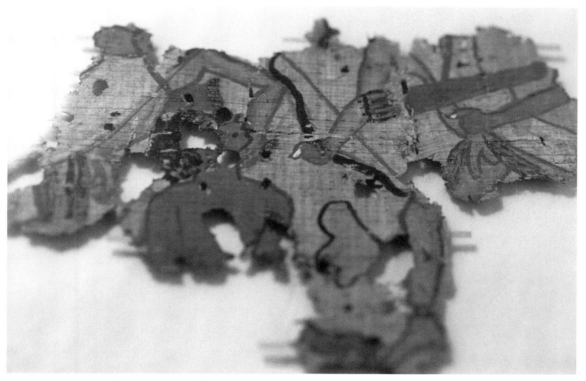

Fig. 102: The Egyptians rarely portrayed the vulnerability of their soldiers on the battlefield. In this exceptional scene a soldier of Amenhotep IV is shown in peril, with his comrades rushing to his aid. The weapon depicted in this scene shows similar features to those of the Egyptian bow. *(Bridget McDermott/British Museum Collection)*

same scene, the archer is shown crouched on the ground, performing an act of subordination.

In scenes from Theban tombs the bow is depicted protected by a shield guard. Double convex bows are frequently revealed; carried by soldiers from Deir el-Bahri, they are often shown protected by leather or fibre wrappings, which are placed around the belly of the bow (Fig. 104). At the Temple of Hatshepsut at Deir el-Bahri, standard-bearers are also armed with bows. The crafting of archery equipment became an established profession and the affiliated techniques have been recorded in artistic representations on the walls of New Kingdom tombs. The crafting of composite bows can be seen in the early tombs of Menkheperasonb (Fig. 101) and Amenmose, captain of the troops, and on stelae that belonged to the chief bowman, Hor.

Egyptian artists almost never depict New Kingdom archers in narrative scenes. In scenes that record the events surrounding the battle of Kadesh archers

Fig. 103: The soldiers at Medinet Habu address the king, Ramesses III:

You are the king who shines upon Egypt. When you rise the two lands [Egypt] live. Great is your might among the enemy. Thy roaring is circling the sun,the shadow of your sword is over the army. The army will march, filled with thy might, your heart is brave and excellent of plan. Amun appears and leads the way. He places every land beneath your feet and your heart is glad forever.

From the tomb of Amenmose (Theban Tomb No. 19), 19th Dynasty. (*Bridget McDermott*)

Fig. 104: Bows carried by archers were often protected by a wrapping that was placed around the string. The temple of Hatshepsut, Deir el-Bahri. *(Bridget McDermott)*

are shown sitting on quarter-stones, stringing their bows. Archers are portrayed providing protective cover during siege operations, and acting as royal bodyguards. They are often shown herding prisoner processions, a traditional theme in Egyptian art that shows the ceremonial act of counting prisoners of war, images that are first identified among the artistic themes of the Old Kingdom. 'Bringing in the prisoner' reveals a ritual practice that has been mistakenly identified by scholars as a childhood game; the practice evidently portrays a fundamental aspect of the warrior's role. The importance of these scenes supersedes archaic warrior themes of cattle counting – the prisoner count, being an essential element of victory, was a practice deeply embedded in the Egyptian military psyche and so often reproduced in artistic imagery.

Although they were commonly portrayed among the ranks of Ramesses III, angular bows, which were carried by princes and charioteers, were obviously considered weapons of great value. At Medinet Habu the angular bow was the predominant weapon assigned to the archer corps. Phalanx archers, who were armed with these weapons, were often shown carrying the bow over one shoulder. At the Temple of Medinet Habu a unique scene shows the issue of angular bows from the temple armoury, where officials would be employed to hand out the traditional weapons of war to the Egyptian army.

Although rare in depicitons of narrative or active engagement, the presence of archers continued to dominate hunting scenes that were always associated with military victories. Archers were also employed as bodyguards for the king, and on occasion they were depicted behind the king's chariot, where they are frequently armed with auxiliary weapons. During direct engagement archers were deployed at the head of the infantry corps to soften up enemy formations. Soldiers were also employed upon the fortress parapet, where they were expected to shoot at enemy lines. In this context, archers are shown protecting foot-soldiers in siege operations; often the artist portrays the archer being shielded by an infantryman as he aims his weapon against the wall of an enemy fort (Fig. 76). Archers are also often shown armed with rope-coils which they wear across the breast. This rope, which appears only in the 20th Dynasty representations was probably used for the binding of prisoners or for the stringing of body parts, for example, ears, hands and genitals that were severed from the enemy.

Arrows

Excavations have produced many examples of ancient arrows and arrowhead finds (Fig. 105). Bronze arrowheads were discovered at a New Kingdom fort, and dated to the reign of Horemheb (1323–1295 BC). New Kingdom arrows were also tipped with iron and bone and were commonly crafted with a reed body, strong and pliant enough to receive an arrowhead and tail feathers. Arrow shafts were designed between 700 and 760mm long, and were often hollow, reinforced by resin, with a tapered wooden tip. At the lateral end of the arrow, the nock was attached to a natural joint in the reed, which was fletched with three rounded feathers, symmetrically disposed around the shaft, and bound with strips of varnish-coated bark. Arrowheads were generally tanged, the tang being longer than the head so that side pressure did not split the reed, which was bound with thread and resin. Barbed arrowheads were also employed by the military. Arrows were designed with tips of stone; additional flints were added to arrowheads as the frontal tip often snapped on striking its mark. There has been much confusion about New Kingdom arrows as a result of erroneous conclusions being drawn as to the specification of their hunting and military functions. Blunt arrowheads have been regarded as hunting equipment, although these arrowheads may be compared with military weapons.

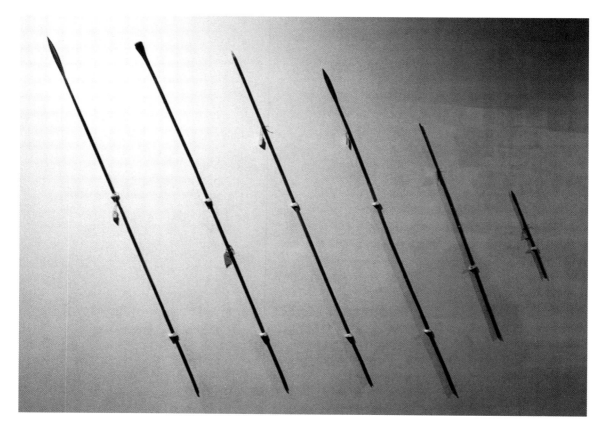

Fig. 105: A wide range of arrows found in the tomb of Tutankhamun. *(Bridget McDermott/Luxor Museum)*

Fig. 106: In this detail from the tomb of Mahu Akhetaten from the Amarna Period, a soldier is shown brandishing a baton shaped in the style of an arrow (below, left). During this time the arrow became a symbol of authority and this type of baton was used by officers. *(Bridget McDermott)*

Collections of arrows discovered in the tomb of Tutankhamun are designed with a wide range of heads which include notched, leaf- and fan-shaped tips along with the blunt wooden arrowhead discussed above (Fig. 105). It is thus difficult to distinguish with any certainty between arrows used by soldiers and those employed for hunting purposes alone.

Bundles of arrows can be seen illustrated in New Kingdom tomb paintings where some groups are shown stored in or bound together with linen strips. This would provide protection for the weapons while supplies were being transported to the field. Archery equipment also appears in scenes which depict offerings, gifts or the payment of taxes. During the New Kingdom, the arrow is adopted as an official emblem, in much the same way that the English adopted the mace and the sceptre as instruments of state ritual (Fig. 106). In an early New Kingdom text it is stressed that Queen Hatshepsut placed her arrow among the Northerners: the arrow symbolised her military domination.

Quivers

During the New Kingdom quivers became elaborate in design; they were decorated with Assyrian motifs and became prized objects of war. They were included in a booty list of Ramesses III, who retrieved 2,310 quivers after his battle with the Libyans. Quivers dated to this period were crafted in soft leather,

Fig. 107: The hood of a quiver that would have originally been attached by a leather thong. The hood and quiver are made of soft leather which was dyed a deep red. It was embossed with beautiful floral designs. The quiver once belonged to a warrior called Mahepera, and was found in his tomb at Thebes. (Bridget McDermott/Egyptian Museum, Cairo)

while a thong was attached to their hoods (Fig. 107). The leather was often dyed and embossed with floral designs. Simple versions of this type have also survived where the quiver is crafted by placing leather over a linen underlay. Quivers that were designed to harbour arrows, staves and javelins were illustrated in the tomb scenes of the New Kingdom where cases often had a square lid. Short quivers, first seen in the tomb of Amenmose, were in common use during the New Kingdom, along with hollow wooden capsules, which have been discovered with their contents. Cases crafted from plant fibres are also known: they were attached to the body by a shoulder strap. Various depictions from Hatshepsut's temple at Deir el-Bahri show soldiers carrying cases in the form of triangular bow boxes.

Fig. 108: In this detail from a Theban tomb the soldiers are armed with a throwstick, a stave and a baton, which is worn around the soldier's body by means of a leather strap. The soldier on the left also carries a triangular bow case. Although they are often shown in military scenes, only one example of a triangular bow case survives. It was found in the tomb of Tutankhamun and is now on display in Cairo Museum. *(Bridget McDermott/ Metropolitan Museum of Art)*

Fig. 109: Various types of quivers are shown used by soldiers at Medinet Habu. These include the traditional cylindrical type (right), a lion-headed stave quiver (centre) and a sack quiver (left). The soldiers also carry triangular bow boxes on slings. *(Bridget McDermott)*

Scenes which show the manufacture of quivers are known from New Kingdom tombs, and the use and manufacture of triangular bow boxes are also revealed in scenes from the tombs of Meri, Kenamun and Huy (Fig. 108). Large numbers of arrows were stored in quivers. A long cylindrical container of leather complete with shoulder strap was capable of carrying as many as eighty arrows.

A differential between the style of quivers used by Egyptian soldiers is best illustrated in the scenes that deal with the battle waged against the Sea Peoples at the Temple of Medinet Habu. Here various types of quiver are distinguished (Fig. 109). Both stave men and archers employ the typical cylindrical case. An ornamental quiver, decorated with lion heads, and triangular bow cases are both carried by soldiers; however, here we see the introduction of a papoose-shaped quiver, which was carried around the shoulder with a sling.

At Medinet Habu the soldiers of Ramesses III are shown armed with long cylindrical quivers that are carried by means of a hand strap. In the tomb of Ibi, a bowman is shown carrying a group of quivers on a sling, and in the tomb of Haremheb a unique scene shows long cylindrical quivers hooked to a carrier. During the New Kingdom, quivers were frequently shown in military scenes on temple walls; detailed images are portrayed, where quiver lids are shown open. At Luxor temple, a mounted horseman is depicted with a quiver; (Fig. 75) this image suggests that mounted warriors were employed within the ranks of the early 19th Dynasty army, although there is evidence that horsemen were used from the Amarna Period onwards.

SOLDIERS AND HATCHETS

During the New Kingdom, hatchets and model axes were included among foundation and funerary deposits. Small axes were probably utilised as toys and were discovered among the goods in child burials. During the New Kingdom, bronze axes were manufactured in stone mould casts, while the blade was forged by hand. Although elongated lugs appear on early 18th Dynasty axes there are many transitions and variations regarding their design. Axes, which gradually adopted shorter lugs and narrow blades, were designed to counteract the developments in enemy armour. The new form, which first appears among excavated remains at Deir el-Ballas, is thought to have replaced the epsilon axe used during the Old and Middle Kingdoms. Symmetrical axes with elongated lugs were first known to have been manufactured at the beginning of the 18th Dynasty; bronze pins secured the blade, while the handle was bound with thongs of hide in order to prevent the wood from splitting. During the late New Kingdom there is evidence that some axes were cast in closed, two-piece moulds and were hafted on to the shaft of the axe rather than vice versa. Generally, the New Kingdom axe was less ornamental than weapons of early periods, although some were engraved. The shaft base or blades of axes often bear royal cartouches or identification marks (Fig. 110). While marching, the soldier suspended the weapon on his body with the help of strapping; during operations, it was often the case that the axe was secured in the back of the kilt, or in the body strap, and it is only during the New Kingdom that the practice of suspending the axe from the shoulder becomes evident. Many axes of this period are clearly pierced – a hole is often bored into the shaft for the application of a leather thong.

The asymmetrical weapon became the major battle-axe of the 18th Dynasty; the earliest blades which were wider at the cutting edge were clearly effective on naked or lightly clothed skin. This type of blade would be held in the wound on impact. It is clear that the narrow axe was designed not only to maim the body, but also to pierce scaled armour. During the New Kingdom, the earliest representations of the soldier and the axe can be dated to the reign of Hatshepsut, and appear on her mortuary temple at Deir el-Bahri (Fig. 62). The axe bears a narrow blade, while the haft is slightly curved. Axes, which were not portrayed but certainly utilised during this period, were also designed with long hafts that were swung with both hands. The excavated remains of hatchets that date to this period correspond typically with their artistic representations (Figs 110 and 62). Subsequently, due in particular to the abundance of axe remains, it has been possible to establish that artistic portrayal with regards to weapons is often highly accurate in execution.

Within the context of Egyptian art, soldiers are also shown in ceremonial or martial settings saluting a superior by pressing the axe against the breast; they are also shown armed with chopping axes which they used to fell trees during siege operations (Fig. 76). Axes were frequently illustrated in the tombs of the nobles. They were shown as tribute to Hatshepsut in the tomb of Dow-er-eneh and in manufacturing scenes from the tomb of Ipuimre and Menkheperrasonb. In the tomb of Ineni, there are several depictions of soldiers wielding axes in non-military contexts. Here an axeman is portrayed in a processional phyle,

Fig. 110: Excavated remains can be compared with ancient images. An axe recovered from Deir el-Bahri may be compared with representations from the same site (see Fig. 62). These axes, inscribed with the name of Tuthmosis III, are from the Egyptian Museum, Cairo. *(Bridget McDermott)*

while a comrade, to whom female prisoners have been consigned, brandishes his axe in threatening gestures above their heads. In the tomb of Antef axes are shown placed in tribute dishes, some are bound and lashed while many appear in blade form. Rows of lashed axes are included, too, in the tomb scenes of Rekhmire. During this period axes bearing the classic skewed form are now tapered to a fine narrow blade with a rounded cutting end. Once this type of axe was established, there was little variation in the type of hatchet used by the military.

Few remains survive from the 19th and 20th Dynasties, and evidence is derived from artistic representations alone. The development of the axe within the 19th Dynasty context of technology and design features elongated lugs, which produced thick and heavy axes. Few soldiers employed within the ranks of the army of Ramesses II are shown bearing axes of this type, although axes with thick wide blades were employed by sappers, who were shown in representations of siege scenes. Variations in the design of axe types shown at Medinet Habu were the result of the introduction of the cast socket hatchet, a type of axe shown in the possession of royal persons. Although they are foreign in origin, axes with cast sockets have been recovered from New Kingdom sites. This type of axe was cast in a two-piece closed mould, rather than the one-piece open mould which the Egyptians had traditionally employed.

Although the Egyptians were familiar with the metal, iron weapons are rare. The first known example of an iron halberd was discovered at a 20th Dynasty site at Abydos. Iron axes were discovered at the Meroitic cemetery at Soleb, while a similar axe was recovered from a disturbed site at the Ramesseum. Iron model axes discovered at Deir el-Bahri share similar features: all have hooked lugs. There are rare examples of the double axe being utilised by ancient Egyptian soldiers.

SOLDIERS AND SWORDS

During the New Kingdom, the true sword was manufactured as a result of the technological innovations accomplished during the Hyksos rule. Developments in New Kingdom metallurgy enabled the Egyptian craftsmen to create long swords with tapered tangs, which strengthened the weapon for military purposes. During combat, stress points were predominately centred on the hilt of the sword and long tangs provided extra stability for a weapon that had previously been manufactured during the Middle Kingdom in separate units (Fig. 111). Early examples of this type of mould cast sword were designed with inlaid handles. Swords intended for the elite soldier were designed with superior and

Fig. 111: A Middle Kingdom short sword or dagger. *(Bridget McDermott/University of Liverpool Museum)*

Fig. 112: Various swords of a New Kingdom date. *(Bridget McDermott/British Museum Collection)*

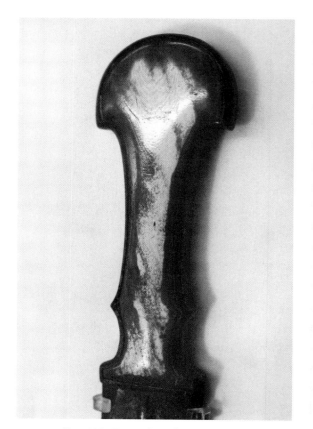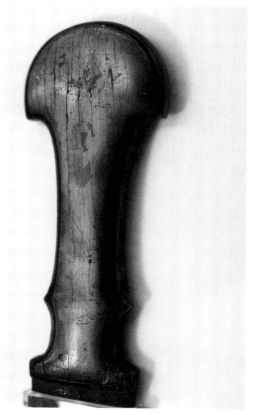

Fig. 113: Two sides of a sword from the British Museum Collection. The sword has an inlaid handle that shows signs of wear. This type of friction often occurs when a weapon is worn on a belt. (Bridget McDermott/British Museum Collection)

elaborate craftsmanship (Fig. 112). They were often inscribed with the king's cartouche, so that when the sword was thrust into the enemy, the iconographical presence of the ruler could be felt. While short daggers were often carried on a band around the arm, swords were kept on a belt around the waist. Friction from this caused the pommels of some long-swords to show signs of wear (Fig. 113). Long-swords, which were usually designed with a sharp double edge, were used as thrusting weapons. The curved sword, or khepesh (Figs 114 and 115) was made to slash and pierce and was often designed with a long inlaid hilt and a light narrow blade. A second version of the khepesh was designed in a single blade of bronze. A long, leaf-shaped sword, cast with a plain or crescent-shaped pommel, was also in use (Fig. 116). While various materials were used for the manufacture of ceremonial weapons, the New Kingdom sword was generally crafted in bronze. Weapons of this type, designed with a leaf-shaped blade, were

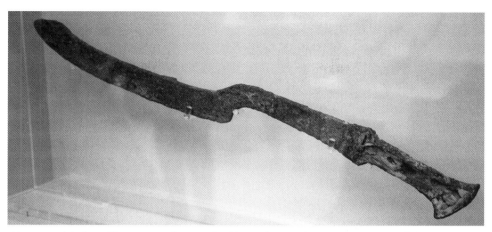

Above and below: Figs 114 and 115: The khepesh sword is a masterpiece of design. It was remarkably light. The bronze sword (below), for example, weighs only 754g. The sword was wielded so that the outer rim of the blade was used to strike the target. (*Bridget McDermott*)

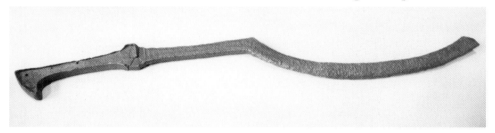

found in the city of Akhetaten (Figs 116 and 117). Although rare, iron weapons have been identified among ancient military arms.

Gods and kings are frequently shown armed with swords. These weapons were occasionally included among the burial equipment of royalty or officials – for example two khepesh swords were found among the contents of the tomb of Tutankhamun. Studies have suggested that the sword reached the height of its importance during the reign of Merneptah; however, the weapon was clearly used by the Egyptian army from the early New Kingdom Period. The earliest examples of the artistic depiction of the soldier and sword can be seen at the Temple of Hatshepsut at Deir el-Bahri, where duelling soldiers are also depicted with short khepesh swords (Figs 118 and 119). These weapons were crafted in wood and used in ceremonial context, when stick-fighting or sword-play was probably enacted among the funeral rites of Egyptian kings. These swords were often crafted with looped handles.

Swords are shown as objects of tribute in the early Theban tombs where foreigners are shown with both the khepesh and straight sword. During the

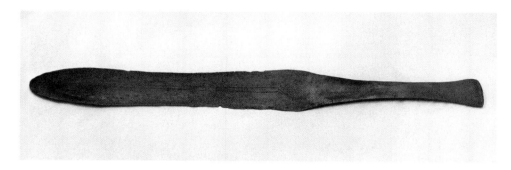

Above and left: Fig. 116: Simple leaf-shaped swords were cast in one mould and were probably used by infantrymen. (*Bridget McDermott/Egyptian Museum, Cairo*)

Fig. 117: In this illustration from a wooden casket found in the tomb of Tutankhamun a leaf-shaped sword is shown being used by the Egyptian soldier. (*Bridget McDermott/British Museum Collection*)

Figs 118 and 119: Although the earliest representation of the khepesh sword appears at Hatshepsut's temple at Deir el-Bahri (below and detail above), another type of duelling sword has also been found at the site. These swords were made of wood and were used during combat displays (left). *(Bridget McDermott/British Museum Collection)*

19th Dynasty and the reign of Ramesses II, long-swords and khepesh swords were both carried by the infantry and are shown among reliefs that depict the siege of Ashkelon and the battle of Kadesh. In some scenes it is common to see soldiers executing the enemy by forcing a straight sword into the breast or throat (Fig. 117). The sword is used in a ceremonial context to show the dismembering of enemy prisoners; these scenes usually include the amputation of hands. Bowmen and members of the king's bodyguard are armed with khepesh swords. In rare battle scenes, groups of khepesh swords are shown abandoned among the casualties of war. Soldiers engaged in siege operations were also armed with the long-sword, as are the soldiers depicted in direct action, while the khepesh is often reserved to non-combatant formations. The khepesh sword is rarely included in scenes which involve violent contact, playing a predominant role in processional or ceremonial scenes (Fig. 9). The khepesh is often carried by soldiers in traditional hunting scenes. There is little variation in the artistic portrayal of the soldier and the sword during the reign of Ramesses III. Its role as a slashing weapon may have proved difficult to execute within the canon of Egyptian art, where the artist traditionally avoided renditions of movement.

SOLDIERS, SPEARS AND JAVELINS

Although there are no extant material remains of spears from the New Kingdom, numerous examples of javelins, which were used as both hunting and military weapons, have survived (Fig. 120). Made of wood and often decorated with strips of bark, they terminated in bone handles that enabled the soldier to jam the weapon into the ground or secure his grip. Although it remained a prized metal, during the early New Kingdom spearheads were sometimes crafted from bronze (Figs 121 and 122).

Spears were included among burial equipment. During the New Kingdom, the gods are seen to adopt spears and javelins as traditional weapons of war and, as images of the war god Reshep became popular, his figure is often shown holding a spear and shield. There is a clear connection between the warlike nature of the gods and New Kingdom royal iconography. Rulers adopt a metaphorical association with various weapons including the spear. Spears, in particular, are often worshipped or revered in various cultures, and imbued with aspects of divine or religious significance. Examinations of a spear cult that became popular in Ptolemaic Egypt have led to suggestions that the practice had early origins. Further, it has been suggested that the spear was associated with emblems found on the mythical mound of creation, when the land of Egypt first emerged from the waters of chaos. The war god Horus also used the spear as a symbol of victory.

Civilians also employed the spear. Farmers, who are known to have used this weapon during periods of unrest, sharpened the blades of their spears with stones, a practice that was probably adopted by soldiers. In ancient stories the spear is recognised as an effective killing weapon, even in the hands of non-military personnel. However, there are few pictorial representations of soldiers using spears outside of their military context. While artistic depictions of soldiers illustrate issues of war and subsequent celebrations of victory, there are rare examples of spear-bearing infantrymen taking part in sport. Archaic imagery first seen on the Hunter's Palette is mirrored in representations of the soldiers of Ramesses III shown participating in a lion hunt at Medinet Habu (Fig. 9). In these scenes they are shown marching along the lowest register in

Fig. 120: Staves and javelins from the tomb of Tutankhamun. The pair at the top of the picture are short duelling javelins. *(Bridget McDermott/Egyptian Museum, Cairo)*

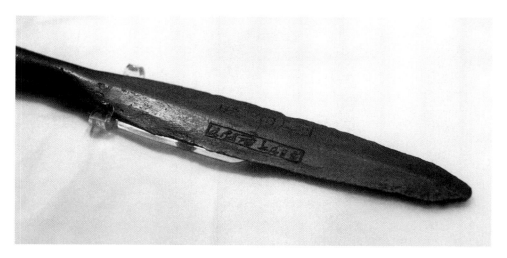

Opposite above and left: Figs 121 and 122: Many weapons, such as these bronze spearheads, were inscribed. *Opposite below*: Fig. 123: Soldiers carrying spears and shields, Luxor Temple. *(Bridget McDermott/British Museum Collection)*

full military regalia. In the same temple, another archaic prototype is revived in the form of a wild bull hunt. Here, infantry were placed behind archer formations (Fig. 103). A rare depiction of a spear can be found on a Ramesside relief fragment that illustrates a man bending over a brazier where he is depicted crafting a weapon of this type (Fig. 104).

It is possible that the javelin was an indigenous weapon, a design that was directly derived from the common spear since the ancient Egyptian prototype bears little resemblance to weapon remains recovered from other Near Eastern countries. The javelin, unlike the spear, was often shown being wielded with aggressive intent. Examples of the remains of javelins discovered in modern excavations are numerous, and many retain bronze blades. The javelin often bears a close resemblance to the Egyptian arrow; indeed, in some late New Kingdom military scenes, they are difficult to distinguish from the latter. Javelins and arrows are similar in design and capability. Both javelin and arrow staffs are often crafted in two sections, the area nearest the point being cut from reed. In some cases javelins are fletched, but the nock is omitted and replaced with a wooden butt. This joint is quite evidently intended to be loose since the butt section, which fitted into the socket, was tapered. Soldiers who are shown wielding javelins are often depicted engaged in hand-to-hand

Fig. 124: A 19th Dynasty workman crafting a spear in relief at Saqqara. (*Bridget McDermott/ Egyptian Museum, Cairo*)

combat, usually as individual combatants dispatching enemy soldiers with one thrust of their weapon, while rare images from this period show enemy soldiers cut down by javelin wounds.

During the New Kingdom period, spears were never illustrated being hurled or dispatched. For this reason scholars have envisaged the spear largely as a thrusting weapon. However, it is clear that the spear had always allowed the soldier to attack with both thrusting and mid-range capabilities. The Egyptian artist faced great difficulties in articulating this type of intention. The artist, restricted by the spatial rationing of the traditional register, preferred to show the phalanx in a static close-range formation (Fig. 123). During the later New Kingdom, when animated action could be recorded on large-scale surfaces, weapons were portrayed in flight.

A fine relief fragment housed in the Brooklyn Museum depicts an early siege scene that includes the image of a soldier climbing a siege ladder with his spear (Fig. 96). The javelin was often depicted as an important offensive weapon; at Abu Simbel it may be seen in use by two soldiers to dispatch the Hittite enemy in scenes from the battle of Kadesh. A scene from the reign of Ramesses III depicts a soldier dispatching a Syrian warrior. This soldier carries his javelin as a single weapon, although a long conical javelin quiver is apparent on his back. In rare scenes from this period, the javelin is utilised not only by infantrymen, but by archers, who carry the weapon with the blade inverted. In a similar scene, a javelin is carried with a shield. The soldier holds the javelin by the grip above his head, while his opposite hand propels the weapon from the extreme of the staff. The javelin is almost always shown being used in close combat: the soldier is often portrayed gripping the extended arm of his enemy in a display of total control, while his javelin was thrust by the opposite hand. On other occasions, tall spears are illustrated amid the phalanx formations, while the chariot units retain the small javelin or pike. However, despite the artistic presentation of the javelin as a hand-held weapon, there is evidence to suggest its use in other contexts. It is probable, for instance, that a special unit of runners used the javelin as a long-range weapon, hurling it over several metres.

SOLDIERS AND STAVES

The Egyptian kings often personified the aggressive attributes of their weapons; in Papyrus Anastasi, for example, Merneptah is identified as the 'beating rod'. Weapons are also often linked to ancient myths and stories. Although clubs of various configurations were used in military contexts, they were also utilised as official or royal accessories, serving as symbols of office, or old age, a tradition that still exists in African tribal culture. The stave was crafted from wood, but examples of bronze and plant fibre clubs are also known; the grips were crafted with rough strips of hide or loops of leather.

Innovations in the design of the stave are most apparent among tomb scenes dated to the Amarna Period. In the tomb of Khons, stick-fighters are presented on the central deck of a military ship engaged in combat (Fig. 125). This theme commonly occurs on boats where pairs of male figures are armed with duelling staves.

During the late Ramesside Period, variations in stave design include an addition of a forked handle (Fig. 73), a type of stave most commonly included among battle scenes of the 19th Dynasty (Fig. 101). It is possible that double or multiple papyri stalks were bound and used during stick-fighting contests. A long, straight stave with a curved head and handle strap can also be identified in depictions of this type of duel (Fig. 69). Short curved batons with and

Fig. 125: Stick-fighters shown on a river boat, in a detail from the tomb of Khons at Thebes. *(Bridget McDermott)*

without butt caps were depicted, while an exceptionally long curved baton (Fig. 103), often shown carried by infantrymen at Medinet Habu, is now on display in the Cairo Museum.

The curved stave was known from the early 18th Dynasty and was depicted among the arms of the heavy and light infantrymen and archers. Serrated staves, sharpened into several slivers of branched wood, are pictured near the Shrine of Hathor at Deir el-Bahri, and a young male seen in a processional scene from the same site is shown armed with this type of weapon (Fig. 119). Variation in the design of the stave can be seen in New Kingdom tombs of Kenamun, where long staves with forked handles and a club that resembles a modern baseball bat are depicted (Fig. 108).

Land soldiers are not generally represented among the military reliefs of Seti I. However, at the Abydos temple of Ramesses II, a pair of soldiers are shown with both straight and curved batons, some of which are carved with lethal notches that were no doubt designed to maximise skull injuries. Soldiers were represented in training scenes from the tomb of Amenmose where they were

Left: Fig. 127: This type of weapon, a mace with a blade, or poleaxe, is rarely depicted. It is shown here in a scene from the tomb of Sennefer in Thebes. The mace in the soldier's hand is crafted to a blade. The weapon was also used by royalty.

Below: Fig. 126: Detail from Karnak temple of a soldier carrying a poleaxe and an epsilon axe (in his hand) and a box (on his shoulder). *(Bridget McDermott)*

armed with fighting sticks. Forked batons continued to be used during the reign of Ramesses II by trumpeters who served in the army. The battle of Kadesh scenes at Abu Simbel show warriors armed with long straight batons. Staves retained their role as an important contact weapon and they were often shown being used to dispatch the enemy. Various types of stave were shown, too, among illustrations of battle-camps. While four soldiers are shown executing Hittites with staves, a chariot runner is armed with the same. The power of the club is emphasised by the manner in which it is grasped. In scenes where soldiers are shown using straight and forked staves to beat confessions from the Hittite spies the blows are directed to the upper body. In similar scenes prisoners are shown being grasped by the hair and struck. In other representations, the enemy is seen placed on the ground between two Egyptians, who beat them with clubs.

There are numerous depictions of the stave among the temple reliefs of Ramesses III at Medinet Habu (Fig. 9). Many variations in stave types were illustrated in single scenes. Phalanx soldiers were issued with both straight and forked handled batons. The appearance of weapons in royal tombs is rare, but forked batons were also depicted in the tomb of Ramesses III. Rounded staves

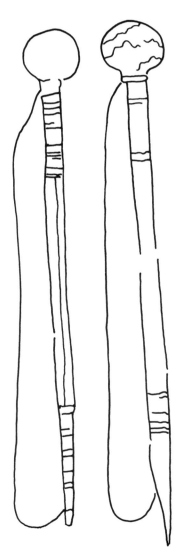

appear in duelling scenes in his funerary temple at Medinet Habu, where the duel may have been a part of the funerary rituals of the Egyptian king (Fig. 69). Here handles are shown attached to the posterior end of the stave, and the soldiers wear jaw-guards to protect themselves from the blows of their opponents. The forked handles of the stave are replaced with leather loops, and the staves are reinforced with leather webbing to aid the warrior's grip. The New Kingdom soldier carried his staves in large quivers that he bore on a strap across his back.

SOLDIERS AND MACE

There are no extant artistic representations of warriors armed with the mace dating from the New Kingdom. Although traditional maces were retained in representation, their design altered in an attempt to counteract developments in enemy scaled armour. For instance, the mace was often depicted with a curved blade (Figs 126 and 127). In the tomb of Rekhmire the mace is shown with a wider shaft, and it also appears on New Kingdom coffin panels where it is shown with a sharpened tip that would also serve to pierce flesh. Examples of maces with body straps have also been

Fig. 128: A mace with a body strap. *(Bridget McDermott/Metropolitan Museum of Art)*

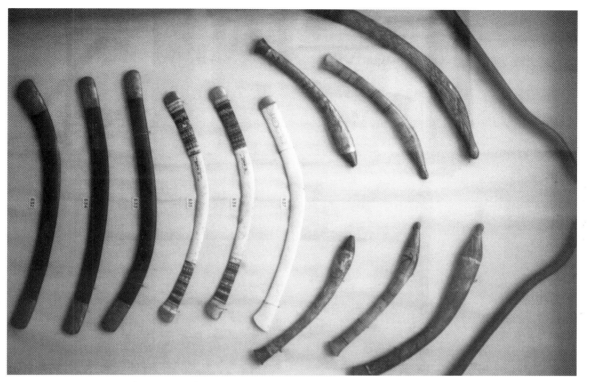

Fig. 129: A wide variety of throwsticks were found in the tomb of Tutankhamun. *(Bridget McDermott/Egyptian Museum, Cairo)*

found. The strap allowed the soldier or hunter to wear the weapon around his shoulder (Fig. 128).

SOLDIERS AND THROWSTICKS

It is clear from literary texts that throwsticks were traded during the reign of Hatshepsut; indeed, they are clearly depicted on the queen's mortuary temple at Deir el-Bahri, where soldiers in processional units carry thowsticks and axes. Deposits excavated from the area outside the tomb of Senmut (an official often described as the favourite of the pharaoh Hatshepsut) include throwsticks that were found among a large and varied weapons collection (Fig. 129).

Appendix I

WEAPONS OF THE AMARNA PERIOD

Armour

Helmets are first shown in the New Kingdom tombs of Kenamun and Seimnewet, a pair of officials who worked under Amenhotep II, the grandfather of Amenhotep III, both dated to the Amarna Period. War inventories of this period indicate that helmets were transported or stored in elaborate boxes, some made of precious stones. A soldier depicted among the ranks of the army of Akhenaten is shown wearing a leather or bronze helmet in a fragmentary representation of the Amarna army from a papyrus in the British Museum collection. It is clear that the helmet is Mycenean in style and scholars have suggested that in this instance the soldiers were mercenaries. However, during a period of immense innovation in the design of armour, it would not be surprising to find that the Egyptian soldier had adopted this type of helmet as a part of his personal defence. Furthermore, it is impossible to distinguish a mercenary element in this representation with any certainty. Evidence suggests that the Egyptian army retained this type of helmet until the 26th Dynasty.

The ancient practice of linen binding, which is still common among the warriors of Africa, served to deflect the blows of offensive weapons and remained popular among the land soldiers of the New Kingdom. This practice is evident in the ranks of Akhenaten's army, where soldiers adopted a short linen garment which covered the upper part of the body and finished with a high abdominal band, leaving the arms and waist exposed. Identical garments are shown being worn by the soldiers of Tutankhamun (Fig. 117). The king's troops are depicted wearing this garment in various styles on the panels and lid of the decorated wooden casket that was found in his tomb. The Egyptian soldier placed the linen material over one shoulder and around the abdomen, leaving the opposite arm and shoulder unprotected. In one example, a soldier is shown having woven the linen around his waist leaving no flesh visible, while another wears linen around the upper body, leaving the abdomen exposed. A single soldier wears no protection of any kind. This type of irregularity in representation may imply that soldiers carried and applied linen to their bodies in various styles, instead of adopting a single garment.

Although the manufacture of metallic armour is known from the reign of Tuthmosis III, coats of scaled armour are illustrated purely as royal garments. However, mail coats were used throughout the Amarna Period, and they continued to be represented in funerary art. During this period, the weight and size of scaled armour dramatically increased leading some scholars to suggest that this type of armour was used on statuary of the period. However, when these scales were examined, fabric remains were identified (Fig. 82). This suggests that even plates of the largest size were sewn on to linen or leather. Although it is clear that scaled armour was retained by the elite, it is important to note that the helmet, which was originally established as a part of the armour of the upper classes, later came to be adopted by the common soldier during the Amarna Period. It is probable that the soldier applied metallic fragments to his uniform for protection during combat. Examinations conducted on several textile fragments from an unprovenanced location at Akhetaten indicate that small leather tags were ribbed, dyed and sewn to imitate scaled armour. These tags were sewn on to the uniform of the police and military divisions. A leather corset of this type was found in the tomb of Tutankhamun. Innovations in the design of armour during the Amarna Period led to a high degree of sophistication in the manufacture of mail coats, reaching a peak during the reign of Tutankhamun and remaining a constant feature of military uniform throughout later periods of Egyptian history.

Lower Body Protection

It is not until the Amarna Period that a reinforced panel is fully established on the front of the kilt to emphasise and protect the genital area (Fig. 83). An early example of this type of kilt is seen worn by a standard-bearer on the left entrance wall of the court of Amenhotep III at Luxor Temple. Although the straight kilt was permanently retained by the military, in scenes of combat and festivity New Kingdom soldiers wore the panelled kilt.

A distinctive feature of the military uniform included the adaptation of a protective panel of leather webbing that was worn around the kilt (Fig. 92). The garment was designed to protect the kilt while the wearer sat on rough surfaces or travelled by boat. Many soldiers are represented wearing them. Webbed loincloths are frequently depicted being worn by the soldiers of Tutankhamun. They are initially depicted on a wooden casket discovered in the king's tomb (Fig. 117), and were worn in both combat and processional displays. This type of kilt was used as a part of the uniform of the soldiers depicted in the tomb of Huy, and of Horemheb's troops who were depicted at his Memphite tomb. It did not feature in late New Kingdom military art.

The Shield

The New Kingdom shield was manufactured with three separate panels of wood, nailed together and covered in hide or simply painted. During the Amarna Period and the later New Kingdom, shields were often strengthened with an embossed bronze disc (Fig. 95), and often decorated with cobras.

It is clear that shields were issued to soldiers by the state. The manufacture and the storage of shields became the responsibility of military officials and, during the New Kingdom, armouries were established at temples and forts in Egypt and abroad. Weapons and arms are shown kept in storage in the tombs of the nobles of this period while the manufacture of shields can be seen in the tomb of Mahu, where hides of the short ovoid style are shown being stretched by workmen over wooden braces. A unique scene from the west wall of the tomb of Panhesy shows a building that may have been used as a shield factory. An armoury situated within the city of Akhetaten is depicted with two floors; it is shown guarded by a sentry who carries a shield slung over his shoulder. During the Amarna Period, there are some innovations in the style of the shield used by the soldiers of Amenhotep III, where a short oval panel is embossed with a tiny disc that is placed in the centre of the shield. It is possible that this stud was made from metal, and may have been used to represent the Aten disc. During this period, regiments were affiliated to their corps through standards, and they can be identified as individual regiments; for example one group is referred to as 'the beloved regiment of the disc'.

Infantrymen on the second register in the tomb of Meryra carry shields that are visibly strapped around the shoulder. Evidence suggests that the shield, spear and axe were the most common weapon in the regalia of the Amarna infantryman (Fig. 123). Although it is unlikely that the common soldier would have used the fine type of shield that was found in the tomb of Tutankhamun (Fig. 97), artists were required by convention to provide their warriors with grandiose weapons and armour. This practice can be seen on the conventional rendering of Tutankhamun's army as it is presented on the painted wooden panels of his wooden casket (Fig. 117). Elaborate images such as these are repeated on the Luxor Temple colonnade. Here, soldiers can be seen participating in the annual Opet festival; this event, which took place at Thebes, was a celebration of the fertility of the land. The shields are identical in appearance to those used by the soldiers of Amenhotep III, having an embossed disc at their centre (Fig. 123).

Bows

During the New Kingdom the design of the Egyptian bow went through various changes; one has only to examine the remains of bows from the tomb of Tutankhamun to appreciate the diversity of design in archery equipment (Figs 88 and 99). Although the self-bow was still retained, the Egyptians had adopted both the Assyrian bow and the Hyksos composite bow. The Assyrian bow was introduced to the archer's regalia during the latter half of the 18th Dynasty; however, remains are rare. During this period stelae were commissioned by bowmen, and became a standard item of funerary equipment.

A number of twisted bowstrings were found in the tomb of Tutankhamun, as well as one example of a linen bowstring with a leather brace; New Kingdom bows were also found in the tombs of Amenhotep III and Tutankhamun (they had been passed down through family members). Composite bows have also been recovered from the tombs of nobles during this period, while double convex bows are shown being carried by footsoldiers who march behind infantrymen. The importance of the role of the archer during the Amarna Period cannot be downplayed. During the reign of Amenhotep III and Akhenaten the archer seems to have been highly revered. Formal greetings to bowmen were included in personal addresses to the king and a keen regard for the welfare of Egyptian archers is evident from foreign correspondence. At this time archers were employed to protect territory affiliated to the crown, and bowmen were often dispatched abroad; indeed, many of the letters addressed to Akhenaten reveal desperate requests for military assistance in the form of Egyptian archers. On arrival at a foreign court, preparations were specifically undertaken to provide board for the Egyptian bowmen. Foreign vassals were held personally responsible for the welfare and even the lives of the king's archers. In a letter to the king, one foreign vassal was forced to defend his position when Egyptian bowmen died under his jurisdiction.

It is evident that archers were regarded as an elite and highly skilled force, who were expected to finish off the enemy, a fact clearly attested in a letter sent to the Egyptian vizier by Rib Hadda, who had requested a dispatch of 200 soldiers in order to fend off the enemy until the archers arrived. It is highly likely that foreigners regarded these elite forces with deep respect. One foreign ruler describes the fear of the enemy: 'if they hear of archers coming out, they will abandon their cities and desert'. Clearly, too, the strength and prowess of the Egyptian bowmen are regularly emphasised: 'And may the archers of the king, my lord, my sun, my god, smash the heads of his enemies'. That foreign rulers made much of the presence of Egyptian bowmen suggests that even a small body of men could deter an attack. It was thought that the appearance of the Egyptian archers could prevent the loss of a city, as if their mere presence imparted a psychological strength that proved invaluable to allied warrior-states.

Arrows

Excavations have produced many examples of ancient arrows and arrowhead finds. However, there is little variation in design during the Amarna Period. Collections of arrows discovered in the tomb of Tutankhamun are designed with a wide range of heads which include notched, leaf- and fan-shaped tips along with the blunt wooden arrowhead discussed above (Fig. 105). A collection of eight arrows housed in the Musée du Louvre also provides a comparative scale of weapons. During this period the arrow had become a potent symbol of authority. In the tomb of Mahu, runners are shown carrying a baton that was crafted in the shape of an arrow indicating that this object had been adopted as a symbol of rank (Fig. 106).

Quivers

Scenes from the Amarna tombs often illustrate crafting techniques, while the use and manufacture of triangular bow boxes are also revealed in New Kingdom tombs. A triangular leather box from the tomb of Tutankhamun in the Egyptian Museum, Cairo is the only surviving example of its kind, and examinations have shown that it was used to transport several bows at one time.

Hatchets

Axes and their binding materials have survived from the Amarna Period. During this period, when the axe was the most common weapon associated with the infantry, artistic representations never deviated from the traditional design and axe shafts were still slightly curved. Although axes are absent from the military reliefs found in the Memphite tomb of Horemheb, it is logical to assume that this weapon was used during his reign. Axes with a slimmer blade were included among the artistic representations featured during the reigns of Tutankhamun and Ay. However, there is also a notable absence of axe remains from the tomb of Tutankhamun. It is astonishing that no hatchets were recovered from the tomb that has produced the world's most definitive collection of ancient weapons.

Mace and Throwsticks

This type of weapon was rarely shown outside the context of royal representation. However, the mace can be seen in the early tomb of Kenamun, where it is shown with a sharpened tip that would also serve as a piercing weapon. The mace also occurs with a body strap so that the soldier or hunter could wear the weapon around his shoulder.

Throwsticks are shown as a part of the arms of the Amarna soldier at Luxor temple (Fig. 123), and here their curvature is moderated. Soldiers are shown with throwsticks on the walls of the tombs of this period and the remains of these weapons are common. Elaborate throwsticks were found in the tomb of Tutankhamun (Fig. 129). Although plain sticks were used, some excavated remains were designed in the shape of snakes.

Spears and Javelins

The spear may be recognised as a weapon of importance when it is illustrated on the stelae of mercenary soldiers from Akhetaten. Spears continued to be used during the Amarna Period. On numerous occasions they are included in foreign tribute and spear types are distinguished in ancient inventories. For instance, a bronze spear believed to have a double overlay of gold was most likely ceremonial. Spears are also recorded among the gifts of foreign rulers such as Tagi and Tushratta, and here bronze weapons are clearly distinguished among plain spears. Subsequently, javelins are also distinguished from the plain spear; being classed as superior arms, they were manufactured with blades of bronze and iron. During this period, there is a perceptible increase in the use of iron in the manufacture of military arms.

From this time there are also many military representations, the majority of which exist in funerary contexts. Spears are represented being stored along with other weapons of war in the armouries at Akhetaten. In a fragment from Akhetaten, spears that are uniform in appearance are depicted in the possession of infantrymen (Fig. 123). They are also shown in readiness for retrieval by soldiers. Spear-bearing infantryman occur in representations of official scenes. Their function was clearly to provide a strong military presence on the occasion of public royal appearances, where they are portrayed in large numbers as bodyguards. In contrast, the common footsoldier was omitted from scenes of religious or official ceremonies. When the presence of the military is recorded in these contexts, the artist identifies only officers and officials.

While the infantry phalanx is always shown with traditional spears, illustrations of hand-to-hand combat present individuals wielding javelins. The clearest indication of the dual use of the spear and javelin can be seen in the representations that occur during the reign of Tutankhamun, where javelins were used in hand-to-hand combat and are clearly depicted in this capacity on a wooden casket found in his tomb. During this time the javelin seems to have been raised to the status of a classical weapon of arms, while duelling and duelling javelins were popularised within artistic themes. A number of these short javelins were included among the funerary goods in the tomb of Tutankhamun (Fig. 120). To dispatch his enemy, a soldier uses the javelin, which is shown being wielded in both hands. In contrast, another scene from the front panel illustrates a phalanx of soldiers carrying plain spears; these spears are about 1.5m in length, with long leaf-shaped tips. The remains of javelins dated to the reign of Tutankhamun or Ay demonstrate the close relationship between javelins and staves. In this case, the javelin was crafted in a traditional fashion and terminated in a wooden grip. However, the weapon was not designed to accommodate a blade, the extremity being pared to a narrow sharpened tip.

The Opet celebration scenes in Luxor temple provide numerous depictions of spear-bearing infantrymen that date to the Amarna Period (Fig. 123). Here, infantrymen are shown proceeding in front of their standard-bearers, and marching in groups of four. The traditional image of infantrymen bearing the shield and spear in one hand is retained.

Staves

Innovations regarding the design of the stave are most apparent among tomb scenes dated to the Amarna Period, when long splayed batons are frequently depicted.

Forked and curved clubs were recovered from the tomb of Tutankhamun, a burial site which produced comprehensive evidence of variation in New Kingdom stave design. Although ceremonial in nature, the staves relate to the type of clubs depicted in the earlier tomb of Kenamun. These include a forked long staff and a club that resembles a modern baseball bat.

Although the straight and forked handled stave remained in use, variations in the type of stave used during the Amarna Period can also be seen in the tomb of Mahu, where soldiers are shown with short clubs and straight batons, some of which have looped straps. In the same tomb four soldiers are shown carrying straight staves. The forked stick was also retained during the Amarna Period; it can be seen in the tomb of Mahu and Huya. However, a unique stave type predominates in the military scenes of the Amarna Period and both infantymen and archers are shown armed with this weapon. Although the subject has rarely been examined, these staves have been variously identified as leather straps, sweeping brooms and even trumpets. It is most likely that these staves were crafted from dried palm fibres which become solid when left in the sun (Figs 80, 83 ad 123). From the tomb of Mahu a group of men is shown armed with these weapons and the Amarna stave is also depicted in the tomb of Meryra and Huya where the curved bludgeon has also been adopted. Although these staves retain their military role during the reigns of Tutankhamun and Horemheb, they disappear from military representations after the latter's rule.

Swords

While various materials were used in the manufacture of ceremonial weapons, the New Kingdom sword was generally crafted in bronze, although iron has been identified among the military arms of this period. A long bronze sword with a leaf-shaped blade was found in the city of Akhetaten, while khepesh swords were found among the contents of the tomb of Tutankhamun. Khepesh swords can also be seen in the tombs of the nobles during this period where they are shown being carried by soldiers or stored as weapons of war. In these scenes they are clearly shown with looped handles. A unique scene from a papyrus dated to this period reveals the vulnerability of an Egyptian soldier who is about to be garrotted by the sword of an enemy soldier (Fig. 102).

Appendix II

LOCATION LIST OF MILITARY REPRESENTATIONS IN EGYPT

The locations of Egyptian military images are significant. Images convey unique insights into the function of Egyptian temples and raise poignant questions about certain aspects of funerary art. The following is a general list of representations examined in this book.

Predynastic Period

Tomb Scenes
Tomb 100: Hierakonpolis
Illustrating stick-fighting; smiting scenes; hunter/warrior themes

Pottery
Illustrating dance/drill; hunter/warrior themes

Weapons
From royal tombs and cemeteries, illustrating staves; bows; mace; quivers

Palettes
Illustrating hunter/warrior themes

Models
Illustrating soldiers on guard

Stelae
Illustrating individual weapons

Old Kingdom

Tombs
Tomb of Meruka
Tomb of Yeduw
Tomb of Khamehesit
Tomb of Inta

Illustrating male initiation rites; stick-fighting; battle scenes (hand-to-hand combat); siege scenes

Weapons
From royal tombs, cemeteries and pots, illustrating hatchets; maces; bows; quivers; arrows

Temple and tomb fragments
Illustrating archers; soldiers in phyle

Middle Kingdom

Tomb Scenes
Tomb of Senbi, Meir
Tomb of Ankhtifi, Moalla

Tomb of Amenemhat, Beni Hasan. No. 2
Tomb of Baqt I, Beni Hasan. No. 29
Tomb of Baqt III, Beni Hasan. No. 15
Tomb of Khety, Beni Hasan. No. 17
Tomb of Knumhetep, Beni Hasan. No. 3
Tomb of Tjeuti-Hetep, El Bersheh.
Tomb 2

Illustrating siege scenes; hunter-warrior
scenes; hand-to-hand combat; fatal
contact; weapon retrieval

Models
Illustrating armed wooden soldiers; soldiers
on river-boats; weapons on river-boats

Jewellery
Various weapons used as amulets

Coffin depictions
A wide variety of weapons are painted
on Middle Kingdom coffins

Human remains
The mummified remains of the soldiers
of Mentuhotpe II

New Kingdom
Royal Tombs
Tomb of Ramesses III (KV 11)
Tomb of Seti I (KV 17)

Illustrating weapons collections;
archers

Private Tombs
Tomb of Kheruef. No. 192
Tomb of Ibi. No. 36
Tomb of Amenhotpe-Si-Se. No. 75
Tomb of Meri. No. 95

Tomb of Menkheperrasonb. No. 42
Tomb of Rehkhmire. No.100
Tomb of Kenamun. No. 93
Tomb of Seimnewet. No. 92
Tomb of Tjauny. No. 74
Tomb of Huy. No. 40
Tomb of Ineni. No. 81
Tomb of Tutu. No. 8
Tomb of Panhesy. No. 6
Tomb of Meryra. No. 2
Tomb of Antefoker. No. 60
Tomb of Kheruef. No. 192
Tomb of Nebamun. No. 90
Tomb of Mahu. No. 9
Tomb of Ipuimre. No. 39
Tomb of Puyemre. No. 39
Tomb of Ay. No. 25
Tomb of Ahmes. No. 3
Tomb of Khaemhet. No. 57
Tomb of Userhet. No. 56
Tomb of Haremheb. No. 78
Tomb of Pentu. No. 5
Tomb of Huya. No. 1
Tomb of Pareneffer. No. 7

Illustrating weapons collections; foreign
presentations of weapons; stick-
fighting; soldiers' hygiene; recruitment
of soldiers

Pottery/Ostracon
Illustrating queen firing bow on chariot;
Reshep with shield and spear

Weapon remains
From forts; foundation deposits; royal
burials; cemeteries; town houses

All weapon types

Models and Votive Objects
Weapons as amulets

Papyri
Illustrating satirical images of battle;
Akhenaten's army

Temple Reliefs
From Deir el-Bahri; Karnak Temple;
Luxor Temple; Abu Simbel; Beit el Wali
Temple; Abydos; Ramesseum; Medinet
Habu

Illustrating siege scenes: on parapets,
attacking the enemy; climbing ladders;
protective cover; cutting down trees;
sapper duties; hunting scenes;
recruitment; bodyguards; dog handlers;
beating scenes; marching phyles, military
musicians; duelling scenes; soldiers in
festival scenes; soldiers in fatal contact –
throat cutting or stabbing; being issued
with arms; supplication scenes; runners;
wrestling (from Amarna), soldiers
engaged in talking/sleeping.

Appendix III

CHRONOLOGY OF ANCIENT EGYPT (AFTER GRIMAL, 1992)

4500–3150 BC: Predynastic Period
4500–4000 BC: Badarian

4000–3500 BC: Naqada I (Amration)
3500–3300 BC: Naqada II (Gerzean A)
3300–3150 BC: Naqada III (Gerzean B)

3150–2700 BC: Thinite Period
3150–2925 BC: 1st Dynasty
3150–3125 BC: Narmer-Menes
3125–3100 BC: Aha
3100–3055 BC: Djer
3055–3050 BC: Djet
3050–2995 BC: Den
2995–2950 BC: Anedjeb-Semerkhet
2960–2926 BC: Kaa

2925–2700 BC: 2nd Dynasty
Hetepsekhemwy
Reneb
Nynetjer
Weneg
Sened
Peribsen
Sekhemib
Khasekhemwy

2700–2190 BC: Old Kingdom
2700–2625 BC: 3rd Dynasty
Nebka
Djoser
Sekhemket
Khaba
Neferkare
Huni

2625–2510 BC: 4th Dynasty
Snoferu
Cheops
Djedefre
Chephren
Baefre (?)
Mycerinus
Shepsekaf

2510–2460 BC: 5th Dynasty
Userkaf
Sahure
Neferkare-Kakai
Shepseskare
Neferefre
Neiserre
Menkauhor
Djedkare-Isesi
Wenis

2460–2200 BC: 6th Dynasty
Teti
Userkare
Pepy I
Merenre I
Pepy II
Merenre II
Nitocris

2200–2040 BC: First Intermediate
    Period
2200–c. 2160 BC: 7th and 8th
    Dynasties
Many short-lived kings

2160–c. 2040 BC: 9th and 10th
Dynasties (Herakleopolis)
Meribre Khety I
Neferkare
Nebkaure Khety II
Neferkare Meribre
Wahkare Khety III
Merikare

2160–2040 BC: 11th Dynasty (Thebes)
Mentuhotpe I
Inyotef I
2118–2069 BC: Inyotef II
2069–2061 BC: Inyotef III
2061–2040 BC: Mentuhotpe II

2040–1674 BC: Middle Kingdom
2040–1991 BC: 11th Dynasty (Unified
    Egypt)
2040–2009 BC: Nebhepetre
    Mentuhotpe II
2009–1997 BC: S'ankhkare Mentuhotpe
    III

1997–1991 BC: Nebtawyre Mentuhotpe
    IV
1991–1785 BC: 12th Dynasty
1991–1962 BC: Ammenemes I
1962–1928 BC: Sesostris I
1928–1895 BC: Ammenemes II
1895–1878 BC: Sesostris II
1878–1842 BC: Sesostris III
1842–1797 BC: Ammenemes III
1797–1790 BC: Ammenemes IV
1790–1785 BC: Sobekneferu

1785–1633 BC: 13th and 14th
    Dynasties
Sekhemnre-Khutawy
Ammenemes V
Sehetepibre II
Ammenemes VI (Ameny the Asiatic)
Hornedjheritef 'The Asiatic'
c. 1750 BC: Sobekhotep I
Reniseneb
Hor I
Ammenemes VII
Ugaf
Sesostris IV
Khendjer
Smenkhkare
Sobekemsaf I
c. 1745 BC: Sobekhotep III
c. 1741–1730 BC: Neferhotep I
Sahathor
Sobekhotep IV
1720–1715 BC: Sobekhotep V
Neferhotep II
Neferhotep III
Iaib
c.1704–1690 BC: Iy
Iny
Dedumesiu I

1674–1553 BC: Second Intermediate
  Period
1674–1553 BC: 15th–16th–17th
  Dynasties
1674 BC: Dedumesiu I
Dedumesiu II
Senebmiu
Djedkare
Monthuemsaf

15th and 16th Dynasties – Hyksos
Salitis
1650 BC: Yaqub-Har
Khyan

17th Dynasty – Thebes
Rahotep
Inyotef V
Sobekemsaf II
Djehuty

1633 BC: End of 14th Dynasties –
  Thebes
Mentuhotpe VII
Nebiryau I
Inyotef VII
Sequenre I
Sequenre II
Kamose

1633 BC: XIV End of Dynasty – Hyksos
Apophis I
Apophis II

1552–1069 BC: New Kingdom
1552–1314 or 1295 BC: 18th Dynasty
1552–1526 BC: Ahmose
1526–1506 BC: Amenophis I
  (Amenhotep)

1506–1493 BC: Tuthmosis I
1493–1479 BC: Tuthmosis II
1479–1425 BC: Tuthmosis III
1478–1458 BC: Hatshepsut
1425–1401 BC: Amenophis II
  (Amenhotep)
1401–1390 BC: Tuthmosis IV
1390–1352 BC: Amenophis III
  (Amenhotep)
1352–1348 BC: Amenophis IV
  (Amenhotep)
1348–1338 BC: Akhenaten
1338–1336 BC: Smenkhare (?)
1336–1327 BC: Tutankhaten –
  Tutankhamun
1327–1323 BC: Ay
1323–1295 BC: Horemheb

1295–1188 BC: 19th Dynasty
1295–1294 BC: Ramesses I
1294–1279 BC: Seti I
1279–1212 BC: Ramesses II
1212–1202 BC: Merneptah
1202–1199 BC: Amenmesse
1202–1196 BC: Seti II
1196–1190 BC: Siptah
1196–1188 BC: Twosre

1188–1069 BC: 20th Dynasty
1188–1186 BC: Setnakht
1186–1154 BC: Ramesses III
1154–1148 BC: Ramesses IV
1148–1144 BC: Ramesses V
1144–1136 BC: Ramesses VI
1136–1128 BC: Ramesses VII
1128–1125 BC: Ramesses VIII
1125–1107 BC: Ramesses IX
1107–1098 BC: Ramesses X
1098–1069 BC: Ramesses XI

Bibliography

Abdel-Kader, M. 'The Administration of Syro-Palestine during the New Kingdom',
  Annales du Service des Antiquités de l'Égypte 56 (1959), 105–37

Adams, B. *Ancient Hierakonpolis*, Warminster, 1974

Adams, W.Y. 'Invasion, Diffusion, Evolution', *Antiquity* 42 (1968), 194–215

Agthe, J. *Waffen aus Zentral-Afrika*, Frankfurt, 1985

Albright, W.F. 'The Israelite Conquest of Canaan in the Light of Archeology',
  Bulletin of the American School of Oriental Research 74 (1939), 11–23

Aldred, C. 'Hair Styles and History', *Bulletin of the Metropolitan Museum of Art* 15
  (1957), 141–7

——. *Egypt to the End of the Old Kingdom*, London, 1965

——. *Egyptian Art*, London, 1980

Alexander, D.G. 'Two Aspects of Islamic Arms and Armor', *Metropolitan Museum
  Journal* 18 (1983), 97–104

Amin, A. 'Ancient Trade Routes between Egypt and the Sudan', *Sudan Notes and
  Records* 51 (1970), 23

Andrews, C. *Ancient Egyptian Jewellery*, London, 1990

Arkell, A.J. 'Throwing-sticks and throwing-knives in Darfur', *Sudan Notes and
  Records* 22 (1939)

——. 'The Prehistory of the Nile Valley', *Handbuch der Orientalistik* (Leiden) VII
  (1975), 1.2

Arnold, D. *Mitteilungen des Deutschen Archäologischen Instituts*, Cairo, 1971

——. 'Der Tempel des Königs Mentuhotep von Deir el-Bahari', Band III,
  *Archäologische Veröffentlichungen des Deutschen Archäologischen Instituts, Abteilung
  Kairo*, Cairo, 1974

Ayton, E. and Loat, W.L.S. *Mahasna*, London, 1911

Baer, K. *Rank and Title in the Old Kingdom. The Structure of Egyptian Administration in
  the Fifth and Sixth Dynasties*, Chicago, IL, 1960

Barthorp, M. *War on the Nile*, Poole, 1984

Bates, O. *The Eastern Libyans*, London, 1914

Baumgartel, E.J. *The Cultures of Prehistoric Egypt I*, Oxford, 1955

——. *The Cultures of Prehistoric Egypt II*, Oxford, 1960

Bissing, F.W. and Kees, H. *Das Re-Heiligtum des Königs Ne-Woser-Re'*, Leipzig, 1923

Blackman, A.M. *The Rock Tombs of Meir*, Vol. 1, London, 1914

——. *The Rock Tombs of Meir*, Vol. 5, London, 1953

Bonnet, H. *Die Waffen der Völker des alten Orients*, Leipzig, 1926

Borchardt, L. *Catalogue général des Antiquités Égyptiennes du Musée du Caire. Nos. 1–1294. Statuen und Statuetten von Königen und Privatleuten im Museum von Kairo*, Berlin, 1911

Botti, G. 'A Fragment of the Story of a Military Expedition of Tuthmosis III to Syria', *Journal of Egyptian Archaeology* 41 (1955)

Brack, A. and Brack, A. *Das Grab des Tjanuni Theben Nr. 74*, Deutsches Archäologisches Institut, Abteilung Kairo, 1977

——. *Das Grab des Haremheb. Theben Nr. 78*, Deutsches Archäologisches Institut, Abteilung Kairo, 1980

Breasted, J.H. *The Battle of Kadesh. A Study in the Earliest Known Military Strategy*, Chicago, IL, 1903

——. *The Edwin Smith Surgical Papyrus II*, Chicago, IL, 1930

——. *Medinet Habu*, 8 vols, Chicago, IL, 1930–32

——. *Ancient Records of Egypt*, 5 vols, Chicago, IL, 1988

Broadhurst, A. 'An Artistic Interpretation of Seti I's War Reliefs', *Journal of the American Research Center in Egypt* 75 (1989), 229–34

Brovarski, E.J. 'Akhmim in the Old Kingdom and First Intermediate Period', *Bibliothèque d'Études* (Cairo) (1985), 97/1, 117–53

Brovarski, E. J. and Murnane, W. 'Inscriptions from the Time of Nebhepetre Mentuhotep 11 at Abisko', *Serapis I* (1969), 11–27

Brunton, G. *Qua and Badari*, Vol. II, London, 1928

——. *Qua and Badari*, Vol. III, London, 1930

——. *British Museum Expedition to Middle Egypt. First and Second Years*, London, 1937

——. 'Syrian Connections of a Composite Bow', *Annales du Service des Antiquités de l'Égypte* 38 (1938), 251–2

Brunton, G. and Caton-Thompson, G. *The Badarian Civilisation*, London, 1928

Brunton, G. and Morant, G.M. *Mostagedda and the Tasian Culture*, London, 1937

Bruyère, B. *Rapport sur les Fouilles de Deir el Medineh*, Cairo, 1924–7

Budge, E.A.W. *The Egyptian Sudan: Its History and Monuments*, Vol. I, London, 1907

Buttery, A. *Armies and Enemies of Ancient Egypt and Assyria, 3200 BC to 612*, Goring on Sea, 1974

Calverley, A.M., Broome, M. and Gardiner, A.H. *The Temple of King Seti I at Abydos*, Vol. IV: *The Second Hypostyle Hall*, Chicago, IL, 1933–58

Caminos, R.A. *Late-Egyptian Miscellanies*, Oxford, 1954

Caminos, R.A. and Fischer, H.G. *Ancient Egyptian Epigraphy and Paleography. The Recording of Inscriptions and Scenes in Tombs and Temples*, New York, 1976

Caneiro, R. 'A Theory of the Origin of the State', *Science* 160 (1970), 1187–92

Capart, J. *Les Debuts de l'Art en Égypte*, Brussels, 1904

——. *Primitive Art in Egypt*, London, 1905

——. 'Note sur la décapitation en Égypte', *Zeitschrift fur Ägyptische Sprache und Altertumskunde* 36 (1989), 125

Carman, J. and Harding, A. (eds), *Ancient Warfare. Archaeological Perspectives*, Stroud, 1999

Carter, H. *The Tomb of Tut'ankh'Amen*, 3 vols, London, 1927–33

——. *The Tomb of Tutankamun*, London, 1972

Case, H. and Payne, J.C. 'Tomb 100: The Decorated Tomb at Hierakonpolis', *Journal of Egyptian Archaeology* 48 (1962), 5–18

Catling, H.W. 'Bronze Cut-and-Thrust Swords in the Eastern Mediterranean', *Proceedings of the Prehistoric Society* 22 (1956), 102–25

Champollion, J. *Monuments de l'Égypte et de la Nubie*, 4 vols, Paris, 1835–45

Cherf, W.J. 'The Function of the Egyptian Forked Staff and One Forked Bronze Butt: A Proposal', *Zeitschrift fur Ägyptische Sprache und Altertumskunde* (1982), 86–97

——. 'Some Forked Staves in the Tutankhamun Collection', *Zeitschrift für Ägyptische Sprache und Altertumskunde* (1988), 115

Chevereau, P. *Prosopographie des cadres militaires égyptiens de la Basse Époque. Carrières militaires et carrières sacerdotales en Égypte du XI au II siècle*, Paris, 1985

Christian, E. 'A Throwstick of Princess Nfr-Nfrw-R'e with Additional Notes on Throwsticks of Faience', *Annales du Service des Antiquités de l'Égypte*, 71 (1987)

Christophe, L.A. 'L'organisation de l'armée égyptienne a l'époque ramesside', *La Revue de Caire* 207 (1957), 387–405

Citola, B. 'Ramses III and the Sea Peoples: A Structural Analysis of the Medinet Habu Inscriptions', *Orientalia* 57 (1985), 275–306

——. 'The Terminology of Ramses III's Historical Records with a Formal Analysis of the War Scenes', *Orientalia* 60 (1991), 9–57

Clark, J.D. 'Interpretation of Prehistoric Technology from Ancient Egyptian and Other Sources, Pt I: Ancient Egyptian Bows and Arrows and their Relevance for African Prehistory', *Paléorient* 2/2 (1974), 323–88

Clastres, P. *The Archaeology of Violence*, New York, 1994

Clausewitz, C. *On War*, 1997

Cline, E. 'Amenhotep III and the Aegean: A Reassessment of Egypto-Aegean Relations in the 14th Century BC', *Orientalia* 56 (1987), 1–35

Cockburn, A.E. (ed.), *Mummies, Disease and Ancient Cultures*, Cambridge, 1980

Collins, L. 'The Private Tombs of Thebes: Excavations by Sir Robert Mond. 1905–1906', *Journal of Egyptian Archaeology* 62 (1976), 18–40

Curto, S. *The Military Art of the Ancient Egyptians*, Turin, 1971

Daressy, M.G. *Catalogue général des Antiquités egyptiennes du Musée du Caire. Nos. 24001–24990. Fouilles de la Vallée des Rois*, Cairo, 1902

Davies, N. de G. *The Rock Tombs of el Amarna*, 6 vols, London (1903–8)

———. *The Tomb of Antefoker, Vizier of Sesostris I, and of his Wife, Senet (No. 60)*, London, 1920

———. *The Tombs of Two Officials of Tuthmosis the Fourth (Nos. 75 and 90)*, London, 1923

———. *The Tomb of Kenamun at Thebes*, New York, 1930

———. *The Tombs of Menkheperrasonb, Amenmose and Another*, London, 1933

———. *Ancient Egyptian Paintings*, Vol. I, Chicago, IL, 1936

———. 'Research in the Theban Necropolis. 1938–1939', *Bulletin of the Metropolitan Museum of Art (New York)* XXXIV (1939), 280–4

———. *Tomb of Rekh-mi-Re'at Thebes*, Vol. II, New York, 1943

Davies, N.M. and Gardiner, A.H. *Tutankhamun's Painted Box*, Oxford, 1962

Davies, W.V. 'An Inscribed Axe Belonging to the Ashmolean Museum, Oxford', *Journal of Egyptian Archaeology* 60 (1974)

———. 'The Origin of the Blue Crown', *Journal of Egyptian Archaeology* 68 (1982)

———. *Catalogue of Egyptian Antiquities in the British Museum: Vll. Tools and Weapons. 1. Axes*, London, 1987

———. *Egypt, the Aegean and the Levant. Interconnections in the Second Millennium* BC, London, 1995

Davies, W.V. and Friedman, R. *Egypt*, London, 1998

Dawson, W.R. 'A Bronze Dagger of the Hyksos Period', *Journal of Egyptian Archaeology* (1925)

Debono, F. and Mortensen, B. 'The Predynastic Cemetery at Heliopolis', *Archäologische Veröffentlichungen des Deutschen Archäologischen Instituts, Abteilung Kairo*, Cairo (1988) 63

De Buck, A. and Gardiner, A.H. *The Egyptian Coffin Texts. IV. Texts of Spells 268–354*, Chicago, IL, 1951

Decker, W. *Sports and Games of Ancient Egypt*, Cairo, 1992

Derry, D.E. 'Mummification', *Annales du Service des Antiquités de l'Égypte* (1942), 235–65

Dodson, A.M. 'The Tombs of the Kings of the Early Eighteenth Dynasty at Thebes', *Zeitschrift für Ägyptische Sprache und Altertumskunde*, (1988) 115

Drews, R. *End of the Bronze Age Changes in Warfare and the Catastrophe Ca. 1200* BC, Princeton, NJ, 1993

Duell, P. *The Mastaba of Mereruka*, Chicago, IL, 1938

Dunham, D. *The Barkal Temples*, Boston, MA, 1970

Dunham, D. and Janssen, J. *Second Cataract Forts. Semna and Kumma*. Vol. I, Boston, MA, 1960

Dyer, G. *War*, London, 1986

Edgerton, W.F. and Wilson, J.A. *Historical Records of Ramses III*, Chicago, IL, 1936

Edwards, I.E.S. 'Lord Dufferin's Excavations at Deir El-Bahri and the Clandeboye Collection', *Journal of Egyptian Archaeology* 51 (1965), 16–28

Ehrenreich, B. *Blood Rites*, London, 1988

El-Batrawi, A.M. *Mission Archéologique de Nubie 1929–1934. Report on the Human Remains*, Cairo, 1935

Elliot, P. *Warrior Cults*, London, 1995

El-Mahdy, C. *Mummies, Myth and Magic*, London, 1989

El-Saady, H. 'The Wars of Seti I at Karnak: A New Chronological Structure', *Studien zur Altägyptischen Kultur* 19 (1992), 285–94

Emery, W.B. *The Tomb of Hemaka*, Cairo, 1938

——. *Excavations at Saqqara 1937–1938. Hor-Aha*, Cairo, 1939

——. *Great Tombs of the 1st Dynasty*, Cairo, 1949

Engelbach, R. and Gunn, B. *Harageh*, London, 1923

Epigraphic Survey. *The Tomb of Kheruef*, Chicago, IL, 1980

Erman, A. and Grapow. H. *Wörterbuch der ägyptischen Sprache*, 7 vols, Leipzig, 1925–55

Faulkner, R.O. 'Egyptian Military Standards', *Journal of Egyptian Archaeology* 27 (1941), 12–18

——. 'The Battle of Megiddo', *Journal of Egyptian Archaeology* (1942), 28–9 2–15

——. 'The Euphrates Campaign of Tuthmosis III', *Journal of Egyptian Archaeology* 32–3 (1946–7), 39–42

——. 'Egyptian Military Organisation', *Journal of Egyptian Archaeology* 39 (1953)

——. *The Ancient Egyptian Pyramid Texts*, Oxford, 1969

——. *The Ancient Egyptian Book of the Dead*, London, 1972

——. *A Concise Dictionary of the Middle Kingdom*, Oxford, 1991

Filer, J. *Disease*, London, 1995

Fischer, H.G. 'The Archer as Represented in the First Intermediate Period', *Journal of Near Eastern Studies* 21 (1962), 50–2

——. 'Notes on Sticks and Staves in Ancient Egypt', *Metropolitan Museum Journal* 13 (1978), 5–32

Fischer-Elfert, Hans-Werner. 'The Sufferings of an Army Officer', *Göttinger Miszellen* 63 (1983), 43–6

Fletcher, A.J. 'Ancient Egyptian Hair: A study in style, form and function', PhD thesis, University of Manchester, 1995

Frankfort, H. *The Birth of Civilization in the Near East*, London, 1951

Frankfort, H. and Pendlebury, J.D.S. *The City of Akhenaten II. The North Suburb and the Desert Altars*, London, 1933

Freedman, L. (ed.), *War*, Oxford, 1994

Fried, M. 'Warfare, Military Organisation, and the Evolution of Society', *Anthropologica* 3 (1961–2), 134–47

Fulco, W.J. 'The Canaanite God Reshep', *American Oriental Society* (1976)

Furneaux, R. *Primitive Peoples*, London, 1975

Gaballa, G.A. 'Minor War Scenes of Ramesses II at Karnak', *Journal of Egyptian Archaeology* 55 (1969), 82–8

Gardiner, A.H. *The Tomb of Huy, Viceroy of Nubia in the Reign of Tut'ankhamun No. 40*, Theban Tombs Series 4, London, 1915

——. 'The Ancient Military Road between Egypt and Palestine', *Journal of Egyptian Archaeology* 6 (1920), 99–116

——. *The Wilbour Papyrus II Commentary*, Oxford, 1948

—— *The Inscriptions of Sinai*, London, 1952

Gardiner, A.H. and Peet, T.E. *The Inscriptions of Sinai*, Pt II, London, 1955

Garstang, J. *The Burial Customs of Ancient Egypt*, London, 1907

Giveon, R. 'The Impact of Egyptian Canaan', *Orbis Biblicus et Orientalis* 20 (1978); Freiburg/Gottingen: Universitatsverlag Freiburg/Vandenhoeck & Ruprecht

Goedicke, H. 'The Campaign of Psammetik II against Nubia', *Mitteilungen des Deutschen Archäologischen Instituts, Cairo* 37 (1981), 187–98

——. 'Sinuhe's Duel', *Journal of the American Research Center in Egypt* 21 (1984), 197–201

——. *Perspectives on the Battle of Kadesh*, Baltimore, MD, 1985

Griffith, F.L. *Inscriptions of Siut and Der Rifeh*, London, 1989

Griffiths, J.G. 'The Interpretation of the Horus-Myth of Edfu', *Journal of Egyptian Archaeology* 44 (1958), 75–85

——. *The Conflict of Horus and Seth from Egyptian and Classical Sources*, Liverpool, 1960

Groenewegen-Frankfort, H.A. *Arrest and Movement. Space and Time in the Art of the Ancient Near East*, Cambridge, Mass., 1987

Gundlach, R. *Sen-nefer. Die Grabkammer des Burgermeisters von Theban*, Berlin, 1986

Gwyn-Griffiths, J. 'Human Sacrifices in Egypt: The Classical Evidence', *Annales du Service des Antiquités de l'Égypte* 48 (1948)

Haas, J. (ed.), *The Anthropology of War*, Cambridge, 1990

Habachi, L. 'The Military Posts of Ramesses II on the Coastal Road and the
    Western Part of the Delta', *Bulletin de l'Institut Français d'archéologie orientale* 80
    (1980), 13–30

Hanke, R. *Amarna-Reliefs aus Hermopolis*, Hildesheim, 1969

Hansen, O. 'On the Greek Graffito at Abu Simbel Concerning the Campaign of
    Psammetichus II in Ethiopia', *Zeitschrift für ägyptische Sprache und Altertumskunde*
    111 (1984), 84

Hardy, R. *The History of the Longbow*, Patrick Stephens, 1992

Hassan, A. 'Stöcke und Stäbe im Pharaonischen Ägypten', *Münchner Ägyptologische
    Studien* 33 (1976)

Hassan, S. *Excavations at Giza*, 10 vols, Cairo, 1932–60

Hayes, W.C. *The Scepter of Egypt*, 2 vols, New York, 1990

Helck, W. *Die Beziehungen Ägyptens zu Vorderasien im 3. und 2. Jahrtausend v. Chr*,
    2nd edn, Wiesbaden, 1971

Hoffman, M.A. *Egypt before the Pharaohs*, London, 1984

Hoffman, M.A., Hamroush, H.A. and Allen, R.O. 'A Model of Urban Development
    for the Hierakonpolis Region from Predynastic through Old Kingdom Times',
    Journal of the American Research Center in Egypt 23 (1986), 175–87

Hoffmeier, J. K. 'Some Egyptian Motifs related to Warfare and Enemies and their
    Old Testament Counterparts', *Ancient World* 6 (1983), 53–70

Humble, R. *Warfare in the Ancient World*, London, 1980

Hurst, A. *Medical Diseases of War*, London, 1941

Israelit-Groll, S. 'The Egyptian Administrative System in Syria and Palestine in the
    18th Dynasty: A Model of High Integrative Level', *Fontes atque Pontes. Eine
    Festgabe für H. Brunner, Ägypten und Altes Testament,* 5 edn, M. Gorg, Wiesbaden
    (1983), 234–42

James, E.H. and Edward, F.W. *An X-ray Atlas of the Royal Mummies,* Chicago and
    London, 1980

James, T.G.H. *British Museum Hieroglyphic Texts from Egyptian Stelae* Pt, I, London,
    1961

——. *Corpus of Hieroglyphic Inscriptions in the Brooklyn Museum*, Vol. I, New York, 1974

Janssen, J. *Commodity Prices from the Ramessid Period. An Economic Study of the Village of
    Necropolis Workmen at Thebes*, Leiden, 1975

Janssen, J. and Janssen, R. *Growing up in Ancient Egypt*, London, 1990

Jaros-Deckert, B. *Grabung im Asasif 1963–1970. V. Das Grab des Jnj – jtj.f. Die
    Wandmalereien der XI Dynastie*, 1984

Jequier, G. *Fouilles à Saqqarah. Deux Pyramides du Moyen Empire*, Cairo, 1933

Kadry, A. 'The Social Status and Education of Military Scribes in Egypt during the
    18th Dynasty', *Oikumene* 5 (1986)

Kanawati, N. *The Egyptian Administration in the Old Kingdom: Evidence on its Economic Decline*, Warminster, 1977

Kaplony, P. *Die Inschriften der ägyptischen Frühzeit III*, Wiesbaden, 1963

Keegan, J. *A History of Warfare*, London, 1993

———. *The Face of Battle*, London, 1996

———. *War and our World*, London, 1998

Keegan, J. and Holmes, R. *Soldiers. A History of Men in Battle*, London, 1985

Keeley, L.H. *War before Civilization: The Myth of the Peaceful Savage*, New York, 1996

Keimer, L. 'Bermerkungen zu altägyptischen Bogen aus Antilopenhörnern', *Zeitschrift fur Ägyptische Sprache und Altertumskunde*, 72–4 (1936), 121–8

Kemp, B.J. and Merrillees, R.S. *Minoan Pottery in Second Millennium Egypt*, London, 1980

Kenedy, D. 'The Composition of a Military Work Party in Roman Egypt', *Journal of Egyptian Archaeology* 71 (1985)

Kern, P.B. *Ancient Siege Warfare*, London, 1999

Kitchen, K.A. *The Third Intermediate Period in Egypt (1100–650 BC)*, Warminster, 1973

———. 'Historical Observations on Ramesside Nubia', *Ägypten und Kush* 13 (1977), 213–26

———. 'Egypt, the Levant and Assyria in 701 BC', *Ägypten und Altes Testament* 5 (1983), 243–53

———. 'Les Suites des guerres libyennes de Ramses III', *Revue d'Égyptologie* 36 (1985), 177–9

Komorzynski, E. 'Uber die Soziale Stellung des Altägypytischen Soldaten', *Annales du Service des Antiquités de L'Égypte* 51 (1951)

Kruchten, J. 'Retribution de l'armée d'après le décret d'Horemheb', *L'Égyptologie* II (1979), 143–8

Kuhlmann, K. and Schenkel, W. *Das Grab des Ibi. Theben Nr. 36*, Berlin, 1983

Kuhnert-Eggebrecht, E. *Die Axt als Waffe und Werkzeug im alten Ägypten*, Berlin, 1969

Lacau, P. *Catalogue général des Antiquités Égyptiennes du Musée du Caire. Nos 28001–28126. Sarcophages antérieurs au Nouvel Empire*, Cairo, 2 vols, 1904

Lauer, J. *Saqqara. The Royal Cemetery of Memphis. Excavations and Discoveries since 1850*, London, 1976

Layton, R. *The Anthropology of Art*, Cambridge, 1991

Leibovitch, J. 'Quelques Nouvelles Représentations du Dieu Rechef', *Annales du Service des Antiquités de l'Égypte* 39 (1939), 145–75

———. 'Un Fragment de stèle dédiée à Rechef', *Annales du Service des Antiquités de l'Égypte* (1940–1), 489–92

Lepzius, C.R. *Denkmäler aus Ägypten und Äthiopien*, 12 vols, Leipzig, 1849–56

———. 'Der Bogen der Hieroglyphi', *Zeitschrift für Ägyptische Sprache und Alterumskunde* 10 (1872)

Lesko, L.H. 'The Wars of Ramses III', *Serapis* 6 (1980), 83–6

Lesquier, J. *Les Institutions militaires de l'Égypte sous les Lagides*, Paris, 1911

Lichtheim, M. *Ancient Egyptian Literature. Vol. I: The Old and Middle Kingdoms*, Berkeley, CA, 1975

———. *Ancient Egyptian Literature. Vol. II: The New Kingdom*, Berkeley, CA, 1976

Lilyquist, C. 'The Gold Bowl Naming General Djehuty: a study of objects and early Egyptology', *Bulletin of the Metropolitan Museum of Art* 23 (1988), 5

Lincoln, B. *Priests, Warriors and Cattle. A Study in the Ecology of Religions*, Berkeley, CA, 1981

Litt, B. and Wainwright, G. A. 'The Egyptian Origin of a Ram Headed Breastplate from Lagos', *Man* 51 (1951)

Littauer, M.A. and Crouwel, J.H. *Chariots and Related Equipment from the Tomb of Tut'ankhamun*, Oxford, 1985

Lloyd, A.B. (ed.), 'Religious Consideration at Qadesh and the Consequences for the Artistic Depiction of the Battle', *Studies in Pharaonic Religion and Society in Honour of J. Gwyn Griffiths*, Egyptian Exploration Society, Occasional Papers 8 (1992)

Lloyd, C. *The Nile Campaign. Nelson and Napoleon in Egypt*, Barnes & Noble, New York, 1973

Loeben, C. 'A Throwstick of Princess Nfr-Nfrw-R' with Additional Notes on Throwsticks of Faience', *Annales du Service des Antiquités de l'Égypte* 71 (1987), 143–51

Lorton, D. 'Terminology Related to the Laws of Warfare in Dynasty XVIII', *Journal of the American Research Center in Egypt* 11 (1974), 35

Lucas, A. *Ancient Egyptian Materials and Industries*, London, 1989

McDermott, S.B. *Ancient Egyptian Footsoldiers and their Weapons. A Study of Military Iconography and Weapon Remains*, 2 vols, Manchester, 2002

McDowell, A.G. *Jurisdiction in the Workmen's Community of Deir El-Medina*, Leiden, 1985

Mackay, E.J.H., Harding, G. L. and Petrie, W.M.F. *Bahrein and Hemamieh*, London, 1929

Mackintosh, J.M. *War and the Doctor*, London, 1940

McLeod, W. *Tutankhamun's Tomb Series III: Composite bows from the tomb of Tutankhamun*, Oxford, 1970

———. *Tutankhamun's Tomb Series IV: Self bows and other archery tackle from the tomb of Tutankhamun*, Oxford, 1982

McManners, H. *The Scars of War*, London, 1993

Manniche, L. *Music and Musicians in Ancient Egypt*, London, 1991

Manuelian, P. 'Studies in the Reign of Amenophis II', *Hildesheimer ägyptologische Beiträge* 26 (1987)

Martin, G.T. *The Royal Tomb at El-'Amarna. The Reliefs, Inscriptions, and Architecture*, Vol II, London, 1975

——. 'A Throwstick of Nefertiti in Manchester', *Annales du Service des Antiquités de l'Égypte* 71 (1987), 15

——. *Hidden Tombs of Memphis*, London, 1991

Massoulard, É. *Préhistoire et protohistoire de l'Égypte*, Paris, 1949

Michailidis, G. 'De la Signification Spéciale de Certaines Armes dans l'Antiquité', *Annales du Service des Antiquités de l'Égypte,* 1947

Michalowski, K. *The Art of Ancient Egypt*, London, 1969

Mogensen, M. 'Ein altägyptischer Boxkampf', *Zeitschrift für Ägyptische Sprache und Altertumskunde*, 57 (1922), 87

Monnet, S.J. 'Forteresses ou villages protégés thinites', *Bulletin de l'Institut Français d'archéologie orientale* 67 (1969), 173–88

——. 'Remarques sur les représentations de la peinture d'Hiérakonpolis (Tombe No. 100)', *Journal of Egyptian Archaeology* 73 (1987), 51–8

Montet, P. *Les scènes de la vie privée dans les tombeaux égyptiens de l'Ancien Empire*, Paris, 1925

Moran, W.L. *The Amarna Letters*, Baltimore, MD, 1992

Morkot, R. 'Violent Images of Queenship and the Royal Cult', *Wepawet* 12 (Summer 1980), 1–9

——. 'Studies in New Kingdom Nubia. I. Politics, economics and ideology: Egyptian Imperialism in Nubia', *Wepawet* 2 (1986), 29–48

Moussa, A.M. and Altenmüller, H. *The Tomb of Nefer and Ka-Hay*, 1971

——. *Das Grab des Nianchchnum und Chnumhotep*, Berlin, 1977

Muhammed, M.A. *Development of Funerary Beliefs and Practices Displayed in the Private Tombs of the New Kingdom at Thebes*, Cairo, 1966

Murnane, W. J. 'The Road to Kadesh: Historical Interpretation of the Battle Reliefs of King Sety I at Karnak', *Studies in Ancient Oriental Civilization* 42 (1990)

——. *Texts from the Amarna Period in Egypt.* Atlanta, GA, 1995

Murray, M. *The Splendour that was Egypt*, London, 1951

Naville, E. *The Temple of Deir el-Bahari*, Vol. III, London, 1913

——. *The XIth Dynasty Temple at Deir el-Bahari,* Pt III, London, 1913

Needler, W. *Predynastic and Archaic Egypt in the Brooklyn Museum*, New York, 1984

Newberry, P.E. *Beni Hasan*, Vol. I, London, 1893

——. *Beni Hasan*, Vol. II, London, 1893

——. *El Bersheh (The Tomb of Tehuti-Hetep)*, Vol. I, London, 1894

——. *Beni Hasan*, Vol. IV, London, 1900

——. *The Life of Rekhmara*, London, 1900

Nicholson, P.T. and Shaw, I. (ed.), *Ancient Egyptian Materials and Technology*, Cambridge, 2000

Nunn, J.F. *Ancient Egyptian Medicine*, London, 1996

Olivova, V. *Sports and Games in the Ancient World*, London, 1984

Page, A. *Ancient Egyptian Figured Ostaca*, Aris & Phillips, 1983

Parkinson, R. *Voices from Ancient Egypt. An Anthology of Middle Kingdom Writings*, London, 1991

Parkinson, R. and Schofield, L. 'Akhnaten's Army?' *Egyptian Archaeology* 3 (1993), 34

Petrie, W.M.F. *Kahun, Gurob and Hawara*, London, 1890

——. *Illahun, Kahun and Gurob* London, 1891

——. *Naqada and Ballas*, London, 1896

——. *Deshasheh*, London, 1898

——. *The Royal Tombs of the First Dynasty*, Vol. I, London, 1900

——. *Diospolis Parva: The Cemeteries of Abadiyeh and Hu*, London, 1901

——. *Abydos Part I*, London, 1902

——. *Abydos Part II*, London, 1903

——. *Abydos Part III*, London, 1904

——. *Hyksos and Israelite Cities*, London, 1906

——. *Gizeh and Rifeh*, London, 1907

——. *Tarkhan I Memphis V*, London, 1913

——. *Heliopolis, Kafr Ammar and Shurafa*, London, 1915

——. *Tools and Weapons*, London, 1917

——. *Prehistoric Egypt*, London, 1920

——. *Tombs of the Courtiers and Oxyrhynkhos*, London, 1925

——. *Ceremonial Slate Palettes*, London, 1953

Petrie, W.M.F. and Brunton, G. *Sedment*, London, 1924

Petrie, W.M.F., Brunton, G. and Murray, M. *Lahun*, London, 1923

Petrie, W.M.F. and Ellis, J. C. *Anthedon*, London, 1937

Petrie, W.M.F., Wainwright, G. A. and Mackay, E. *The Labyrinth of Gerzeh and Mazghuneh*, London, 1912

Phillips, G. B. 'The Antiquity of the Use of Iron', *American Anthropologist* 26 (1924), 175–84

Poliakort, M.B. *Combat Sports in the Ancient World*, New Haven, CT, 1987

Porter, B. and Moss, R.L.B. *Topographical Bibliography of Ancient Egyptian Hieroglyphic Texts, Reliefs and Paintings. I. The Theban Necropolis*, Oxford, 1989

Quibell, J.E. *The Ramesseum*, London, 1898

——. *Hierakonpolis*, Vol. II, London, 1902

——. *Catalogue Général des Antiquités Égyptiennes du Musée du Caire. Nos. 11001–12000 and 14001–14754. Archaic Objects*, Cairo, 1905

——. *Excavations at Saqqara 1908–1910*, Cairo, 1912

Quibell, J.E. and Hayter. A.G.K. *Excavations at Saqqara. Teti Pyramid, North Side*, Cairo, 1927

Quirke, S. *The Administration of Egypt in the Late Middle Kingdom. The Hieratic Documents*, Guildford, 1990

Randall-MacIver, D. and Mace, A. *El Amrah and Abydos*, London, 1902

Randall-MacIver, D. and Woolley, C. *Buhen*, Philadelphia, PA, 1911

Ray, J. 'A Pious Soldier: Stele Aswan 1057', *Journal of Egyptian Archaeology*, 73 (1987), 129

Redford, D.B. *History and Chronology of the Eighteenth Dynasty of Egypt: Seven studies*, Toronto, 1967

——. *Akhenaten: The Heretic King*, Princeton, NJ, 1984

——. 'Egypt and Western Asia in the Old Kingdom', *Journal of the American Research Center in Egypt* 23 (1986), 125–43

——. *Pharaonic King-lists, Annals and Day-books. A Contribution to the Study of Egyptian Sense of History*, Toronto, 1986

Reeves, C.N. *The Complete Tutankhamun*, London, 1990

——. *Valley of the Kings: The decline of a royal necropolis*, London, 1990

Reeves, N. and Wilkinson. R.H. *The Complete Valley of the Kings*, London, 1996

Reisner, G.A. 'Work of the Expedition of the University of California at Naga Ed-Der', *Annales du Service des Antiquités de l'Égypte* 5 (1904), 105–9

——. *Catalogue Général des Antiquités Égyptiennes du Musée du Caire. Models of Ships and Boats*, Cairo, 1913

Reymond, E.A.E. 'The Origin of the Spear I', *Journal of Egyptian Archaeology* 49 (1963), 140–6

——. 'The Origin of the Spear II', *Journal of Egyptian Archaeology* 50 (1964), 133–8

——. 'The Cult of the Spear in the Temple at Edfu', *Journal of Egyptian Archaeology* 51 (1965), 144–8

Ricke, H., Hughes, G.R. and Wente, E.F. *The Beit El-Wali Temple of Ramesses II*, Chicago, 1967

Rocatti, A. 'Les Papyrus de Turin', *Bulletin de la Sociéte Française d'Égyptologie* 99 (1984), 9–27

Saad, Z.S. *Royal Excavations at Saqqara and Helwan, 1941–1945*, 1947

Saleh, M. and Sourouzian, H. *The Egyptian Museum, Cairo*, Cairo, 1987

Sandars, N.K. *The Sea Peoples: Warriors of the Mediterranean*, London, 1985

Sandman, M. 'Texts from the Time of Akhenaten', *Bibliotheca Aegyptiaca* 8 (1938)

Säve-Söderbergh, T. *Private Tombs at Thebes*, Oxford, 1957

—— (ed.). *Temples and Tombs of Ancient Nubia*, London, 1987

Schäfer, H. *Priestergräber und andere Grabfunde vom Ende des Alten Reiches bis zur Griechischen Zeit vom Totentempel des Ne-User-Re*, Leipzig, 1908

——. 'Weiteres zum Bogenschieben im alten Ägypten', *Orientalische Literaturzeitung* 34 (1931)

——. *Principles of Egyptian Art*, Oxford, 1974

Scharff, A. 'Vorgeschichtliches zur Libyerfrage', *Zeitschrift für Ägyptische Sprache und Altertumskunde* 61 (1926)

——. 'Some Prehistoric Vases in the British Museum', *Journal of Egyptian Archaeology* 14 (1928), 261–76

Schulman, A. *The Military Establishment of the Egyptian Empire*, Chicago, IL, 1958

——. *Military Rank, Title and Organization in the Egyptian New Kingdom*, Berlin, 1964

——. 'Some Observations on the Military Background of the Amarna Period', *Journal of the American Research Center in Egypt* 3 (1964), 51

——. 'The Nubian War of Akhenaton', *L'égyptologie. Axes prioritaires de recherche, Colloques internationaux du CNRS*, Paris, Vol. II, 1982, 299–316

——. 'Chariots, Chariotry and the Hyksos', *Journal for the Study of Egyptian Antiquities* 10 (1980), 105–53

——. 'The Battle Scenes of the Middle Kingdom', *Journal for the Study of Egyptian Antiquities* 12 (1982),

——. *Ceremonial Murder and Public Rewards. Some Historical Scenes on New Kingdom Private Stelae*, New York and Tel Aviv, 1986

Scott, N. 'The Metternich Stela', *Bulletin of the Metropolitan Museum of Art*, 9 (1950), 201

Seligmann, C.G. and Murray, A.M. 'Upon an Early Egyptian Standard', *Man* 11 (1911), 165

Selim, H. *Excavations at Saqqara. 1937–1938. I . The Mastaba of Neb-Kaw-Her*, Cairo, 1975

Seth, K. *Urkunden des ägyptischen Altertums*, Leipzig, 1906

Shaw, I. *Egyptian Warfare and Weapons*, London, 1991

——. 'Battle in Ancient Egypt: The Triumph of Horus or the cutting edge of the temple economy', in A.B. Lloyd (ed.), *Battle in Antiquity*, London, 1996, pp. 239–69.

Simpson, W.K. 'An Egyptian Statue of a Phoenician God', *Bulletin of the Metropolitan Museum of Art* 10 (1951–2), 183–7

Sliwa, J. 'Some Remarks Concerning Victorious Ruler Representations in Egyptian Art', *Forschungen und Berichte* 16 (1974), 97–117

Smith, E. and Dawson. W.R. *Catalogue général des Antiquités Égyptiennes du Musée du Caire. Nos. 61051–61100. Egyptian Mummies*, Cairo, 1924

Smith, H.S. *The Fortress of Buhen. The Inscriptions*, London, 1976

Smith, R.W. and Redford, D.B. *The Akhenaten Temple Project*, Vol. I, Warminster, 1976

Smith, W.S. 'The Origin of Some Unidentified Old Kingdom Reliefs', *American Journal of Archaeology* 46 (1942), 509–31

——. *A History of Egyptian Sculpture and Painting in the Old Kingdom*, Oxford, 1949

——. *The Art and Architecture of Ancient Egypt*, Harmondsworth, 1981

Spalinger, A.J. 'Some Notes on the Battle of Megiddo and Reflections on Egyptian Military Writing', *Mitteilungen des Deutschen Archäologischen Instituts* 30 (1974), 221–9

——. 'Esarhaddon and Egypt: an Analysis of the First Invasion of Egypt', *Orientalia* 43 (1974), 295–326

——. 'A Critical Analysis of the "Annals" of Thutmose III', *Journal of the American Research Center in Egypt* 14 (1977), 42–54

——. 'A New Reference to an Egyptian Campaign of Thutmose III in Asia', *Journal of Near Eastern Studies* 37 (1978), 35–41

——. 'Egyptian-Hittite Relations at the Close of the Amarna Period and Some Notes on Hittite Military Strategy in North Syria', *Bulletin of the Egyptological Seminar* I (1979), 55–90.

——. 'The Northern Wars of Seti I: An Integrative Study', *Journal of the American Research Center in Egypt* 16 (1979), 29–47

——. 'Historical Observations on the Military Reliefs of Abu Simbel and Other Ramesside Temples in Nubia', *Journal of Egyptian Archaeology* 66 (1980), 83–99

——. 'Notes on the Military in Egypt During the XXVth Dynasty', *Journal of the Society for the Study of Egyptian Antiquities* II (1981), 37–58

Spencer, A.J. *Catalogue of Egyptian Antiquities in the British Museum V. Early Dynastic Objects*, London, 1980

Spring, C. *African Arms and Armour*, London, 1993

Steindorff, G. *Aniba*, 2 vols, Hamburg, 1935–7

Strudwick, N. *The Administration of Egypt in the Old Kingdom*, London, 1985

Thabit. T.H. 'International Relations of the Sudan in Napatan Times', *Sudan Notes and Records* 40 (1959), 19

Thompson, H. (ed.), *A Family Archive from Siut*, Oxford, 1934

Time Life Books. *The Way of the Warrior*, Alexandria, VA, 1993

Tirard, H.M. 'The Soldiers of Ancient Egypt', *Journal of Egyptian Archaeology* II (1915), 299–333

Tobin, V.A. 'Divine Conflict in the Pyramid Texts', *Journal of the American Research Center in Egypt* 30 (1993), 93

Touny, A.D. and Wenig, S. *Der Sport im alten Ägypten*, Leipzig, 1969

Trigger, B.G. 'The Narmer Palette in Cross-cultural Perspective', *Ägypten und Altes Testament* I (1979), 409–19

——. 'Egypt and the Comparative Study of Early Civilizations' in K. Weeks (ed.), *Egyptology and the Social Sciences*, Cairo, 1979, pp. 23–56

Trigger, B.G., Kemp, B.J., O'Connor, D. and Lloyd, A.B. *Ancient Egypt: A Social History*, Cambridge, 1983

Tylecote, R.F., *A History of Metallurgy*, London, 1976

Vandier, J. *Mo'alla. La Tombe d'Ankhtifi et la Tombe de Sébekhotep*, Cairo, 1950

——. *Manuel d'archéologie égyptienne I: Les époques de formations. La préhistoire: les trois premières dynasties*, Paris, 1952

——. *Manuel d'archéologie égyptienne II: Les grandes époques. L'architecture funéraire*, Paris, 1955

——. *Manuel d'archéologie égyptienne III: Les grandes époques. La statuaire*, Paris, 1958

——. *Manuel d'archéologie égyptienne IV: Bas-reliefs et peintures, scènes de la vie quotidienne* I, Paris, 1964

——. *Manuel d'archéologie égyptienne VI: Bas-reliefs et peintures, scènes de la vie agricole à l'Ancien et au Moyen Empire*, Paris, 1978

Velde, H.T. *Seth, God of Confusion*, Leiden, 1967

Vercoutter, J. 'Ancient Egyptian Influence on Sudan', *Sudan Notes and Records* 40 (1959), 8

Virey, P. *Le Tombeau de Rekhmara*, Paris, 1989

Vogelsang-Eastwood, G. *Pharaonic Egyptian Clothing*, Leiden, 1993

Von Bissing, F.W. *Das Re-Heiligtum des Königs Ne-Woser-Re*, 3 vols, Leipzig, 1905–28

Ward, W.A. *Egypt and the East Mediterranean World. 2200–1900 BC. Studies in Foreign Relations during the First Intermediate Period*, Beirut, 1971

Weeks, K. *Egyptology and the Social Sciences*, Cairo, 1979

——. 'An Historical Bibliography of Egyptian Prehistory', *American Research Center in Egypt* 6 (1985)

Weinstein. J.M. 'A 19th Century Egyptian Naval Base?', *Bulletin of the American School of Oriental Research* 238 (1980), 43–6

Wendorf, F. *The Prehistory of Nubia*, Vol. I, Austin, TX, 1968

Wertime, T.A. and Muhly, J.D (eds), *The Coming of the Age of Iron*, New Haven, CT and London, 1980

Western, A.C. and McCleod, W. 'Woods Used in Egyptian Bows and Arrows', *Journal of Egyptian Archaeology* 81 (1985), 77–94

Wild, H. *Le Tombeau de Ti*, Cairo, 1953–66

Wildung, D. *Sudan. Ancient Kingdoms of the Nile*, Paris, 1997

Wilkinson, C.K. 'Egyptian Wall Paintings', *Bulletin of the Metropolitan Museum of Art* 36 (1978–9), 1–56

Wilkinson, G. *Arms and Armour*, London, 1978

Winlock, H.E. 'The Egyptian Expedition. 1935–1936', *Bulletin of the Metropolitan Museum of Art* 32 (1937), 3–39

———. *Excavations at Deir El-Bahri 1911–1931*, New York, 1942

———. *The Slain Soldiers of Neb-hepet-Re Mentuhotep*, New York, 1945

Winlock, H.E. and Mace, A. *The Tomb of Senebtisi*, New York, 1916

Wise, T. and McBride. A. *Ancient Armies of the Middle East*, London, 1981

Wolf, W. 'Über einige Waffen im Berliner Ägyptishen Museum', *Zeitschrift für Ägyptische Sprache und Altertumskunde* 61 (1926), 98–104

Wreszinski, W. *Atlas zur altägyptischen Kulturgeschichte*, 2 vols, Leipzig, 1923–35

Yadin, Y. 'Egypt's Earliest Penetration into Asia', *Israel Exploration Journal* (1955), 1–16

———. *The Art of Warfare in Biblical Lands*, Tel Aviv, 1963

Yeivin, S. 'Amenophis II's Asiatic Campaigns', *Journal of the American Research Center in Egypt* 6 (1967), 129

Yoyotte, J. and Lopez, J. Review [Shulman, A. (1964)]. *Bibliotheca Orientalis* 26 (1969)

Yurko, F.J. 'Merenptah's Canaanite Campaign', *Journal of the American Research Center in Egypt* 23 (1986), 189–215

———. '3,200-Year-Old Picture of Israelites Found in Egypt', *Biblical Archaeology Review* 16 (1990), 20–38

Zadok, R. 'On Some Egyptians in First-Millennium Mesopotamia', *Göttinger Miszellen* 26 (1977), 63–8

———. 'On Some Egyptians in Babylonian Documents', *Göttinger Miszellen* 64 (1983), 73–5

Index